The Art of Balancing Priorities
Between Work and Home

A MAN'S WORK IS NEVER DONE

DAVID Z. NOWELL

Publishers since 1798

THOMAS NELSON PUBLISHERS
Nashville • Atlanta • London • Vancouver

Published in Nashville, Tennessee, by Thomas Nelson, Inc., Publishers, and distributed in Canada by Word Communications, Ltd., Richmond, British Columbia, and in the United Kingdom by Word (UK), Ltd., Milton Keynes, England.

Unless otherwise noted, Scripture quotations are from the NEW KING JAMES VERSION of the Bible. Copyright © 1979, 1980, 1982, Thomas Nelson, Inc., Publishers.

Scripture quotations noted NIV are taken from the HOLY BIBLE, NEW INTERNATIONAL VERSION ®. Copyright © 1973, 1978, 1984 by International Bible Society. Used by permission of Zondervan Bible Publishing House. All rights reserved.

The "NIV" and "New International Version" trademarks are registered in the United States Patent and Trademark Office by International Bible Society. Use of either trademark requires the permission of International Bible Society.

Scripture quotations noted KJV are from The Holy Bible, KING JAMES VERSION.

Library of Congress Cataloging-in-Publication Data

Nowell, David Z.
    A man's work is never done : the art of balancing priorities between work and home / David Z. Nowell.
    p. cm.
    ISBN 0-7852-7878-8
    1. Men—Religious life. 2. Men (Christian theology) 3. Business ethics.
  4. Parenting—Religious aspects—Christianity. I. Title.
BV4843.N68   1995
248.8′42—dc20
                                              94-47652
                                                   CIP

Printed in the United States of America

1 2 3 4 5 6 7 — 01 00 99 98 97 96 95

CONTENTS

PREFACE

Not *another* book on the changing role of men in contemporary society! Well, no, not exactly. This book does address how we as men fit into the big picture, but it does so from a very particular standpoint, with a very certain objective in mind. It seems that most writings today, Christian or secular, that deal with "male issues" (what a terrible phrase) do so from a single-issue orientation. We are told, for example, that the source of tension for today's man is the inability to get in touch with his "inner child." Or, conversely, our problems stem from a refusal to grow up. Or, we have trouble relating to our wives because we as men speak to exchange information, while women talk to form relationships. Or, since we never resolved childhood sexual stereotyping, we can't escape repressed roles. Or, well, the list could go on and on.

There are, however, a lot of good books out there. Books that genuinely attempt to grapple with the issues that men face every day. And many of those works were invaluable resources as this manuscript was prepared.

What seems to be missing from the Christian man's bookshelf, however, is a work that pulls it all together, something that says, "Here's how everything is integrated into a meaningful and coherent whole." That is what I am attempting here. It seems that, if the Christian faith is really about a new birth and a new identity, all that we are ought to be shaped and formed by the reality of our faith. This is not about some super Christianity. I'm not sure what that is. Rather, this is a study of normative Christianity, that real faith that permeates and integrates all that we are.

Father, businessman, husband, churchman. Separate identities? No. Rather, separate roles subsumed under the identity called "Christian." If these roles are pulled together under one identity, there may be tension between the parts we play, but there will not be an ultimate and fatal dissonance. This book is not a promise that "we can have it all." Rather, it is an affirmation that everything in our lives must be brought under the lordship of Christ.

Before I began the research that led to this writing, I must admit that I was somewhat disheartened over what seemed to be the disintegration of the role of Christian men in contemporary America. It was a very pleasant surprise to discover that there are many men in our society who have this thing figured out. They understand what it is to surrender all of their lives to the demands of the gospel. They are actively living their faith in the homes, offices, and churches of America. Christian manhood may not be nearly as far gone as has been reported.

Faith in the marketplace and in the home is not a lost art. Every day, in Fortune 500 companies, in family businesses, on small farms and in large factories, Christian men take their faith into the workplace, then return home each evening and lead their families, by teaching and example, into deeper relationships with Jesus Christ. This book is about that kind of faith. Faith that constantly calls to repentance and builds toward righteousness. Faith that is forever a guide for living.

I know that kind of faith is out there because I encountered it in so many lives. I knocked on the doors and rang the telephones of men all across corporate America. The men whose stories populate these pages were extraordinarily open and honest with me. They willingly reflected on the experiences, values, and choices that shaped not only them, but also their corporations, families, and churches. Without their insight, this book could never have been written.

In addition to the men you will meet in the following chapters, a number of individuals merit specific mention for their help in this project. Cass Fritz brought the concept to life when he suggested it would be extremely helpful to look at the lives of some men who showed a real understanding of the issues. Likewise, Tom Purdy and Dr. Milton Cunningham provided a great service by pointing me toward that very type of individual. Their help in identifying corporate leaders who have integrated the Christian faith into the workplace was invaluable.

My editor, Lonnie Hull DuPont, and all of the staff at Thomas Nelson proved once again to be worthy companions in the odyssey of writing. They are distinguished by their professionalism.

I cannot imagine anyone surpassing my wife Susan in the ability to proof, critique, and generally prepare a manuscript. She deserves, but would not accept, the designation of co-author. Our Jinnifer and Meredith were, as always, sounding boards and willing critics.

Finally, this writing might never have been completed were it not for my brother-in-law, Charles Means, whose pride in craftsmanship provided a wonderful, hand-knotted cotton hammock to which I daily escaped with a load of books and writing pads to compose this manuscript.

To all these, a heartfelt "Thank you."

David Z. Nowell
August 1994

CHRIST OF THE WORKPLACE, CHRIST OF THE HOME

Time keeps on slipping, slipping, slipping, into the future.
noted theologian Steve Miller

June and Ward were not my parents. Still, like most children of the fifties and sixties, I was raised in a fairly typical middle-class family. My mother worked, but she was usually home by the time school was out. Our streets were safe; a Saturday bicycle ride across town took me to my best friend's home. We could spend the day exploring without needing to check in every few minutes. Little League was requisite, as were summer church camp and Friday night football games. The family ate dinner together almost every evening. And if Mom and Dad weren't in the same bed together, it meant that one of them was either in the hospital or at a church retreat of some type.

No, my parents may not have been Ward and June, and yours probably were not either, but they certainly looked a lot more like the Cleavers than my wife and I do. We no longer do family the way it was done only a few decades ago. So many members of our generation have discovered that the traditional home is either not a possibility or, at least, not a priority. We find ourselves desiring to affirm traditional values and longing for the days when family meant warm cookies after school, yet we are trapped by the demands of contemporary society—demands on our time, on our freedom, and ultimately, on those values which somehow seem out of place in this new context.

So, we are all left with a balancing act. The Little League schedule still sits on the kitchen counter, but right beside it is the Delta Airlines flight book. Dad's goodnight kisses are often delivered from the office, if not long-distance from another city. We read a Bible story at breakfast which teaches us that true happiness comes from returning good for evil, then we race to the office to close the deal before a competitor beats us to it. And our children take in all this, leaving us to wonder why they have not developed all the same standards and values that we had when we were children, and we cannot understand why there seems to be a tension in our marriages that our parents never knew.

■ ───────────────────────────────────

The greatest thing in this world is not so much where we stand as in what direction we are going.
—Oliver Wendell Holmes

─────────────────────────────────── ■

I cannot, and the same almost certainly applies to you also, cannot be the same type of husband and father that my father was. Well, that is not entirely true; I have chosen a lifestyle which effectively precludes me from living the life my father lived. It is not, to be sure, a choice always freely made; contemporary society strongly pushes me in that direction. But it is a choice. There is no mandate that a man find success in the business community; we are not legislatively required to return a high standard of living for our families. But most of us choose to participate in that search for success and prosperity, a search that often gets in the way of what is mandated—if not legislatively then at least ethically and most certainly biblically—to be a good husband and father.

We could turn our backs on these contemporary standards of success and just walk away from it all. No more boardrooms, no high-pressure sales, no long hours at the office. It is attractive, but that choice brings its own set of problems—not the least of which is putting food on the table. Besides that, it certainly does not seem that the men who are so ready to indict the business mentality are doing much better with their families; their moral superiority has not made it to the next generation.

[Some fathers] seem to spend their whole lives giving their children a reason to be glad when they are gone.   —Jean de La Bruyère

---

And so each day we return to the office, determined that we can have it both ways. But can we? Can the life of faith exist alongside life in the midst of contemporary society? Ultimately, it may come down to an even more basic question: Do the values of the marketplace destroy the morals of the home? Or, perhaps, can we play the game in the world of business and still be husband, father, and churchman?

Balancing Act

This may be a book of nostalgia, because it is about old-fashioned values in present society. But if it is nostalgia, it is an eyes-wide-open variety, fully recognizing that the marriage of the Christian family to the contemporary workplace is an uneasy alliance, albeit a necessary one. This is not a study in, as some have termed it, "capitalistic propaganda." It is understood that within the coupling of Christianity and commerce, there must always be a tension, a recognition that fully living the ethics of Christ is immeasurably more difficult in the work-place—and that the way we live at the office shapes and forms, to no small extent, our relationships at home. A balancing act, yes, but one in which we feel compelled to participate.

This is a work of affirmation, a confession if you will, that a man can be in the world but of the family. Many of us remain convinced that "Dad" must mean more than the one who provides the paycheck (or, more appropriately today, a portion of the family income). There must be a place in today's world to have a measure of success in business and still fulfill the biblical edict that a man's first concern must be his family. And throughout our world we find men who have struck just that balance which allows them respect from their business peers even as they grasp and actuate the whole of what it means to be a Christian husband and father.

Changing Roles in a Changing World

This is not a book that would have needed to be written a century or even fifty years ago. Ethical dilemmas have, of course, been part and parcel of every man's life. Dealing fairly with others and doing business with integrity, all the while asking, "Who is my neighbor?" were as important at the beginning of the first century as they are at the end of the twentieth. There probably was not, however, the explicit tension that seems to call us to make a choice between financial success and success in the home.

For the first two centuries of the United States' existence, the structure of commerce was such that it largely supported and reinforced what we would today call family values. This was primarily an agrarian society. Work very well may have meant long hours, from sunrise to sunset, but they were hours with sons and daughters alongside.

Even for urbanites, society was still structured in a way which reinforced the role of the man in relationship with his family. Dad might spend long hours at the factory or behind the desk at the bank. But the children understood that his hard work put food on the table for them, and he was home every night, and rarely a stranger to his children as many fathers are today.

That is not to say that there was no trouble in paradise. The paternalism of bygone days certainly had many negative features. The right and responsibility of women to full partnership in the home was often subjugated on the altar of male dominance. Children may have learned right and wrong, but without the freedom to question, they may never have had the opportunity to understand the deeper biblical truth of living in relationships. Still, society allowed the father a role in the lives of his wife and children which is often denied today.

By the midpoint of this century, however, society and the family itself had changed. The family farm, where Dad and the kids could walk out the back door and be at work, had given way as the principal point of commerce to the industrial and business concerns that dominate the urban landscape. The very nature of work had undergone a dramatic transformation.

Even at that juncture, however, men were, for the most part, still full participants in the rites of family. Evenings usually meant the newspaper after supper, while the kids played or finished up homework. Saturdays were taken with Little League games or perhaps a drive to the mountains. Sunday, of course, meant that the family would be together in church.

But something happened in the seventies and eighties. *Time* became a different type of commodity, far more precious than anything traded on the Chicago Board. As the industrialized society has reached maturity—though futurists once told us that automation, robotics, and computers would so reduce the necessity of our labors that our greatest challenge would be determining what to do with our leisure time—we find that the days simply do not contain enough hours to get everything done at the office, much less to attend to the maintenance of relationships at home.

The new hero of the workplace is the man who can log the most hours. Just look at the men portrayed in literature. In John Grisham's *The Firm*, the attorney who is held up as the ultimate model for the new associates is the one who billed a client for twenty-seven hours in one day—by beginning the morning in the eastern time zone then flying to California and adding three hours to his day! We all respect the coworker who never takes a lunch break. Hours behind the desk have become the new standard of masculinity.

And so, some become absentee fathers, choosing to put the hours in at the office at the cost of losing those same hours at home with the family. Many men feel that is a choice in which their hands are tied. The greatest obligation the father has, they argue, is to see that material needs are met, that there is bread on the table, even if that means all other important aspects of being husband and father become secondary or even tertiary.

Changing standards in society have also contributed to this ever-diminishing role men play in the family. Many of those changes were long overdue, and we must welcome them. At the same time, even welcome alterations in society require difficult adjustments. Ease of transition has nothing to do with necessity of change. Many men are left questioning the importance (or the existence) of their role in the home.

When faced with such uncertainty, most men turn to one of two options. Some reject in totality the modern world, seeking the order of a simpler time when the lines were much more cleanly drawn. Or, conversely, they find that it becomes easier to retreat to the male's *sanctum sanctorum*—his office—than it is to make the difficult transitions into new identities.

Neither of these choices is a viable option for the modern Christian man. To be sure, some communities have very successfully turned their backs on the modern world and propagated nineteenth- or even eighteenth-century values. The Pennsylvania and Indiana Amish communities come to mind. But that brings its own set of questions and challenges. For most of us, returning to that type of lifestyle would by no means be the best situation for our families.

Many more men opt for the second alternative. Confused by the changes in the home and in society, we move toward the place where things are much more black and white. In the office, lines of responsibility and authority are usually very clearly drawn. We know what is expected of us, and we have concrete ways to measure our success. Most of us find greater comfort living in the world of black and white than we do in one where competing tensions draw us from side to side. Because the cost of neglecting the home does not show up on a ledger sheet, we do not notice how the penalty we have exacted from the family begins to add up.

To reject the home for the office is an alternative fraught with peril for both the family and society as a whole. It has long been proclaimed from the pulpit, and it is beginning to be acknowledged by sociological and psychological chroniclers of society, that a moral malaise has infected the western world. Some have even suggested that we have begun an "amoral era," when questions of right and wrong are considered irrelevant to the course of action. But, for the great majority of people, such questions remain very much an issue, and we are disheartened by what may be the moral collapse of our society.

Both those on the right and the left are pointing to weakened family structures as the genesis of this loss of morality. More and more, we recognize that the lack of parental, and especially paternal, involvement in the lives of children is a prime source of the dysfunctionalism that marks our culture. If we are to leave our children any hope for the future, it will come only when fathers step in and become involved in the full scope of family life.

We cannot lay this foundation for the future, however, by refusing to engage the modern world and the demands of commerce. If we do, society will say that a choice has to be made: you can either be a father and husband or you can be a businessman, but you cannot be both; these are mutually exclusive roles.

And many men who do not have a strong Christian ethos which calls them to minister to their families will choose to leave the family to its own designs, and a terrible toll will be exacted from our world.

Hokey-Pokey Christianity

When I was in graduate school, my mentor, Dr. C. W. Christian, related a parable from his own life experience which serves well as a lesson for the modern man seeking participation in both the business world and the family. On an afternoon fishing excursion to a friend's pond, he stepped from the dock into a small rowboat. The boat, unloosed from its moorings, immediately began to slip away while Dr. Christian had one foot still resting upon the dock.

As the gap widened between the boat and the dock, and the angle formed by Dr. Christian's legs moved from acute to obtuse, he relates that the thought passed through his mind, "This is what it means to be a believer in the modern world. We find ourselves struggling to keep one foot planted in the reality of our faith, while we risk all by placing the remainder of our weight on the uncertain footing that is our modern world."

Strange man, that Dr. Christian; few of us reflect on the verities of life at moments like that. Even his thoughts immediately returned to the more mundane as he was unceremoniously deposited in the drink. Nonetheless, the point is well-taken: there is risk in engagement. But to engage as the Bible says we must makes such risky activity requisite.

In the midst of that obligation, who of us does not feel a sensation of imbalance as we seek to maintain the precarious perch that engages both worlds? Every time I climb into the car for the drive to the airport, I do so with a pang of separation, knowing that by my absence, I may miss out on a pivotal moment in the lives of my children. I will never forget the Sunday evening a few years ago when my youngest child called me on my car phone to tell me that she had asked Christ to be Lord of her life. While I was overjoyed at the news, her announcement was tainted with at least a passing regret that I had not been there to participate in the moment.

But the roles of businessman and father remain integral to the very identity of many of us today. The tasks are more than just not mutually exclusive. From a biblical standpoint, they are interrelated and cosupportive. My business experience makes me a better father; the support of home and family allows me to be effective in the office.

My pastor, Dr. Ken Massey, has what may be an even better analogy for the believer, what he calls "Hokey-Pokey Christianity." You remember the Hokey-Pokey, that dance you had to do in primary school, the one that started "You put your right hand in; you take your right hand out. . . ." The last verse of that little number calls for us to "Put your whole self in," which is precisely the gospel edict for our lives. We must totally immerse ourselves in all of the tasks to which we are called. To live the life of faith, we must practice a Hokey-Pokey Christianity.

"If You Don't Live It, You Don't Believe It"

A friend handed me a book. "If you are writing about Christianity in the marketplace, you need to know about Marion Wade." The book, The Lord Is My Counsel, *recounts the life story of Mr. Wade, who built a multi-million-dollar company from a simple carpet cleaning service—and did so while maintaining the highest principles of biblical morality. For Wade, there was no separation of confession and activity. As he says in his story, "If you don't live it, you don't believe it."*

There is no parcelling out of our person; we do not give part of ourselves to home, part to the church, and part to the office. Instead, we integrate all these aspects into our lives, giving ourselves fully to each of them. You are at all times a businessman, at all times a husband and father, at all times a churchman. That's Hokey-Pokey Christianity. A central truth of the gospel is this: the same Christ who is Lord of the gospel, who calmed the seas and fed the five thousand, is also Lord of both the home and the office. Only by the integration of all that we are into a composite whole under his lordship can we be all that God calls us to be.

The Search for the Model

During my college years, I served as youth pastor for a church in Houston. At one point the youth group attended a seminar which discussed basic family structure. The seminar leader regularly referred to "the biblical model for the family." The father was seen as the wage earner, and received spiritual and material authority directly from God. The father answered to God, the mother answered to the father, and the children answered to their mother. It was all a neat and concise package.

As I sat in the seminar and looked around at the youth group, I realized that for about half of the group, such a family structure was not even a possibility. Some came from single-parent homes, others were from step- or blended families, and while the others fit within the two-parent, traditional, nuclear family mold, personalities and abilities meant that the model might not be most effective for their families. Yet here we were, hearing that if families wanted to be "within the center of God's will" then the model presented was the only possibility for them.

It certainly seems that even a cursory examination of Scripture reveals a biblical imagery far richer than any cut and dried model. Even in biblical times, families—spiritual, effective families—came in a variety of shapes and forms. But, it does seem that a certain connecting thread ran through all their successes.

One of the most telling examples of familial success in all of Scripture is the story of David and Bathsheba, and they certainly do not fit the model. David saw Bathsheba, the wife of a Hittite warrior named Uriah, bathing on her roof. He sent for her, and they initiated an adulterous affair. Later, finding that their union had resulted in a pregnancy, he had her husband murdered in battle. David then took Bathsheba as one of his wives in order to hide their sin. Shortly before the child's birth and close-following death, David was confronted with his sin by the prophet Nathan. David's lament and plea for forgiveness is recorded in the beautiful and moving fifty-first psalm.

If that were the end of the story, we would be confronted with only the tragedy of sin. But the story does not stop there. David and Bathsheba had a second son and called him Solomon. Under his rule, God gave Israel its greatest national period. The family certainly did not fit the model, but God met them where they were and blessed and used them.

What is the common thread that we see throughout the treatment of the home in Scripture, in the stories of Samuel, Timothy, Moses, and even Ruth and Boaz? The strand that remains unbroken is the reality of God's provision whatever our circumstance may be. None of the families in the stories fit the model, yet God still found effective ways to use these families and to minister to them.

In our world today, few families can match the stencil. If we then hold that model up as the only biblical way to go about being a Christian family, we may disqualify a majority before that quest to be what God wants us to be has even begun.

This issue is really decided by the way we see God. For many, God is seen as the removed lawgiver, a God who passed out the rules and then retired to heaven. If that is who God is, then our range of acceptable possibilities for relational forms is going to be pretty narrowly drawn. We will understand God's will in a very static sense; that is, the course of our lives has been previously charted and it is up to us to discover that pathway and adhere forever to it. There is no room for multiple paths, nor provision for mistakes. The difficulty with such a view is that, if we ever make a wrong turn, the path may be forever lost for us.

Such a view of God does not seem to be the biblical picture. Instead, Scripture draws a God constantly interacting and interloving with his creation, forever meeting us within our brokenness and fallenness and forever making new provision for us. And thus, wherever in life he finds us, God still has a plan for our lives. Perhaps this is why David spoke of *paths* of righteousness.

This is not to say that all the alternatives which we may choose fit within the purview of God's will. Many men, and many who call themselves Christians, do both business and family in ways clearly outside of what God intends for his followers. No amount of rationalization about separating our business from our faith, or about "just trying to do what is right for my family," can change that fact.

At the same time, however, many men are finding new and creative ways effectively to fulfill the call of God in their lives, a call which they are convinced incorporates both their business schedule and their time at home. Most would not even consider themselves the avant-garde in theology. Yet, they are blazing a spiritual path for the many to follow.

One of the great stories which came out of the 1993 NFL season was that of David Williams, an offensive tackle for the Houston Oilers. Williams stayed with his wife during her time of labor and the birth of their child—and consequently missed the team flight to a pivotally important game. To one of the press questions about the example that he had set for the men of America, Williams responded that he did not choose his course of action in order to be a role model. He just did what he thought best for his family. Oh, and by the way, that choice cost him more than $100,000 in salary.

There are many men out there who have become models; some intentionally, some not. For them, the quest to incorporate Christ into all that they do is an ongoing journey, one without an ultimate end, but one whose reward is in the search itself. It is even one whose result may never be seen in this generation, but whose richness is in the travel itself. It is a journey whose success is measured, not in dollars, but in the legacy it leaves.

■ ———————————————————————————

The American lives even more for his goals, for the future . . . Life for him is always becoming, never being. —Albert Einstein

———————————————————————————— ■

This book is a celebration of that journey, both of its triumphs and its trials. We will be accompanied on our travels by some men who have discovered at least a part of the map. Some of them are well-known men like Truett Cathy, the founder of Chick-fil-A, who sets a company standard for morality and fair play. Men like Dale Jones, President of Halliburton, who carries his faith into the marketplace. Men like Ansel Condray, Executive Vice President of Exxon, U.S.A., who understands that faith and living can never be separated. Others may be less well known, but nonetheless have recognized an important guidepost; men like Chuck Staley, Director of Real Estate Programs at Anderson University, whose career choices are constantly informed by the effect they have on his family. And men like Don Elliott, perhaps the world's greatest auto dealer, whose management skills have not only allowed him to shape a prospering and growing company, but have also brought him success as a parent.

So join us for this quest, a new "search for excellence," as we seek to be all that God has designed us to be.

Integrating Faith and Practice

S. TRUETT CATHY
Founder, Chairman of the Board, and CEO, Chick-fil-A, Inc.

I can remember the first time I walked into a Chick-fil-A. That's a bit unusual in itself—I do not remember my first trip to McDonald's or Burger King—or even to Commander's Palace or Brennan's, for that matter. But I *do* remember my first trip to Chick-fil-A because it was apparent that it was like no other restaurant. There was a genuine difference in the demeanor of the employees and the way they approached their jobs.

After a bit of investigation, I discovered that Chick-fil-A had been founded by a Christian gentleman whose understanding of biblical principles drives not only his private life but his business as well. Truett Cathy's principles are an unabashed part of the corporate philosophy.

Perhaps what sets Chick-fil-A apart is a sense of service, rooted not entirely in a profit motive but in a conviction of the spiritual value of the stewardship of giving to others. Mr. Cathy states, "Everything was created for the purpose of giving. All of creation was made to render to other people, whether it is the trees, the ocean, or us as people.

"Everything we do in terms of our corporate philosophy and our corporate goals is set within the standards of biblical principles." Indeed, reading through the corporate principles, you get a real sense of their basis, especially when you reach the final principle:

"Stewardship: We strive to be good stewards of all that is entrusted to us . . . our time, talents, treasures, and natural resources. We believe the best decisions are made with a long-term perspective."

Cathy really doesn't hide his company's "hidden" agenda. Every increase in sales allows him the opportunity to expand his commitment to social ministry toward the youth of America. Cathy has provided almost $10 million in college scholarships through Chick-fil-A restaurants. His WinShape Centre Foundation provides full co-op scholarships to Berry College in Rome, Georgia, for qualified students. His foster care programs maintain seven different foster homes in Georgia, Alabama, Tennessee, and Brazil, providing needy children with a positive family environment.

Cathy is also concerned about the working environment for his employees. Chick-fil-A has, from its inception, maintained a closed-on-Sunday policy. "We want to give our restaurant operators and their employees time to worship if they so choose and time to be with their families."

But, as *Entrepreneur* magazine described him in a 1992 article, "Don't get the idea that Cathy is a Bible-toting evangelist bent on converting the world to Christianity. Cathy is the first to say he respects people's differences—all the more reason to run his business according to ethical and moral principles." No, ". . . this man with a gentle smile is not selling religion, but humanity."

But that still did not tell me how Cathy got all of those teenagers who staff the counters in his stores to be so pleasant. "I guess that comes from the top down. We foster an atmosphere in Chick-fil-A of caring and concern for one another in service to our customers. I think our employees know that we really care about them. And they show that concern for other people. Plus, while we certainly don't have a 'Christians only' hiring policy, we do look for those young men and women who are involved in their schools and involved in their communities and show a genuine care for others."

As you enter the corporate headquarters of Chick-fil-A in Atlanta, you see the corporate purpose etched in stone: "To glorify God by being a faithful steward of all that is entrusted to us, and to have a positive influence on all who come into contact with Chick-fil-A." With a philosophy like that, perhaps the demeanor of the employees should be no surprise.

FATHER KNOWS BEST OR MARRIED WITH CHILDREN?

2

All the world's a stage,
And all the men and women merely players;
They have their exits and their entrances,
And one man in his time plays many parts.
William Shakespeare
As You Like It, Act 2, Scene 7

During my preadolescent years, my father and mother employed their best parenting skills in an attempt to inoculate me against the dire consequences of peer pressure and conformity. To hear the parental litany, this affliction gave rise to all sorts of dysfunctionalism. It was the prime cause of everything from acne to teenage pregnancy. Their warnings were largely ineffectual; during high school in the seventies, I looked pretty much like every other teenage boy in America. My hair length fell within acceptable standards. I dressed like the typical child of suburbia, listened to the same music, and watched the same television shows as my friends.

Perhaps, however, there was some degree of, if not inoculation, at least insulation. Most middle-class adolescents in our

small town did not really face the genuine evils which are associated with teen peer pressure. Alcohol and substance abuse,
sexual promiscuity, and general adolescent thuggery were never
really a part of the standard patterns of behavior for me and
my friends.

What was picked up from those parental discourses was the
idea that this pressure was something that only teenagers faced.
I can remember looking forward to becoming an adult and
being in the "real world" so that some of the minor vices that
were a part of my life due, I thought, to conformity would be
easy to eradicate. Such, it seems, is a common perception of
the nature and timing of peer pressure.

But the demand that we conform is by no means confined
to our teen years, nor is it exerted only by those we perceive
to be negative influences. Indeed, insistence upon compliance
to communal norms pervades the adult Christian community.
And that is not always bad. In fact, even in our teenage years,
such pressure was more a positive influence than it was the road
to perdition. Part of the reason my friends and I never were
consumed by the all-too-prevalent demons of adolescence was
that it was never acceptable behavior in our crowd to get drunk
or be promiscuous. The demand for conformity served, if not
as rudder, at least as a keel in our lives that helped us maintain
some sense of balance and perspective about who we were and
where we were going.

Part of the genius of the New Testament church is its construct of built-in accountability. One of the reasons that we
insist that "Christian" marriages take place if not in the church
building at least within the context of the community of faith,
is so that husband and wife stand accountable both to each
other and to the church. It is a form of peer pressure designed
to bring about right behavior. In the same way, support groups
such as Alcoholics Anonymous provide a type of positive peer
pressure. The desire to conform can be exploited as much for
good as it can be for evil.

For those immersed in the business community, the world is so vastly different today than it was during the days of our youth. Nowadays we want our children to make their own decisions, but we expect those decisions to please us.

Life was much easier for my parents: they knew what a child was supposed to do, and he had jolly well better do it. But things are different with us. We want our children to live according to their own lights, to develop their personalities in freedom, because we believe in freedom and know that coercion is bad. At the same time we want their development to lead to goals we have set for them . . .

There is nothing new, of course, about parents wanting to do right by their child. What is new is that we have grown very afraid of doing wrong by our children . . . —Bruno Bettelheim
Dialogues With Mothers

Not Exactly What I Had in Mind

Even within the community of faith, however, the overt tension to conform to specific life models and modes of behavior can have deleterious effects. Too often, the boundaries of the Christian life are so narrowly constructed that many are excluded by the circumstances of life before they even begin the journey.

Our homes—and especially our roles therein—look nothing like the family we once envisioned we would lead. In high school, and probably into college, most young men develop at least a vague portrait of the lifestyle they anticipate. Despite protestations decrying marriage and family in favor of a "free" single lifestyle, most young men construct an envisioned world that is amazingly Cleaverish: a doting wife, two obedient children, a house in the suburbs, and the family gathered around the dinner table each evening.

For most American families of the nineties, that vision never found fruition. Families, it seems, rarely look like we are told they should. Indeed, almost half of all families do not even meet the traditional definition, with a husband, wife, and children. A whole panoply of new terms has taken our vocabulary: single parent, stepfamily, blended family. And even those families that do qualify for the traditional nomenclature find that realizing the material portion of the dream—middle- to upper-class suburbia—may mean that the relational and spiritual aspects of the family are sacrificed.

Think of how things have changed. For most of our generation, for example, breakfast and dinner were family time. If my father missed a morning or evening meal, it was an exceptional occasion. Mealtime meant the sharing of the day's activities, plans, and news. Thereby, everyone was incorporated fully into the sphere of familial concerns. We children understood well the lives and agendas of our parents because the conversation of the table was, consciously or not, a time of forging bonds.

Not so today. Most children of corporate executives understand that Dad will be at the office a night or two each week. Clients are more frequent dinner companions than are our families. A father's goodnight is often delivered over the cellular phone or from another city. That is not how it was supposed to be. Just a decade or two ago they told us that the biggest problem for the nineties would be deciding what to do with all of the excess time that higher productivity and office automation would bring us, but I've yet to meet the businessman who complains about having too much time!

These times are different, and what it means to be *Father* in this day of new family, community, and world structures, in this day of shrunken time, is vastly different from what it meant

A Daily Dose of Reality

In A Passion for Excellence, *Tom Peters and Nancy Austin report that, three mornings a week, the executives of Castle, Inc. find a 5" x 7" yellow sheet of paper on their desks. The sheet is titled "Daily Dose of Reality." It contains the phone number of a customer who has bought a piece of equipment within the previous six weeks. The manager is required to contact the customer just to see if the customer is satisfied with the equipment. The purpose of this exercise is threefold: 1) to let customers know they are important, 2) to uncover problems before they become major irritants, and 3) to give managers a daily reminder of where the real world is.*

Any management system that keeps those objectives in the forefront will go far toward success. Come to think of it, substitute family for customers and Dad for managers, and any father who maintains these standards will go a long way toward managing the vagaries of family life as well.

to be Father only a generation ago. The reality of the role of father and husband has changed more in the last forty years than it did in the previous three hundred. And from all appearances, that evolution is not anywhere near complete.

Yet, in the midst of a changing and diverse world, contemporary prophets are still describing and prescribing a single model that we are all to follow. We hear it proclaimed from the lecture circuit and from many pulpits. The nuclear family, we are told, with the man constantly in the place of authority and decision making, is the only one that can possibly meet the biblical edict. The diagrams explain just how it is to be done.

If the issue of nontraditional families or families whose circumstances prevent patricentrism are mentioned, it seems to be always in a passing remark to "exceptional (and thereby inferior) cases."

But for millions of American families, the traditional is not a possibility, and the exceptional is the norm. All of these families are told, implicitly if not explicitly, that some kind of spiritual and familial second best is their lot in life, that they can never move into the top tier of God's intent for the family.

We readily recognize that the traditional family is *one* model, and perhaps it is the preferred model, but I never cease to be amazed at how many people—especially those who should know better—are quick to put God in a box and prescribe very tightly the types of situations in which his will can be realized. But those of us who do not fit the model feel a great deal of pressure to conform to a standard which is simply unattainable. And that peer pressure can be as devastating as anything we ever experienced as teenagers.

Make no mistake, this is not a book that says "having it all"—career, family, and church—comes easily, nor even that we may find full realization in all those areas of our lives. This book is an affirmation, however, that God is bigger than the realities of our existence and that, within those realities, he can work to bring new and creative responses to the challenges that mark our way.

■ ────────────────────────────

If you want to know how a family should look, just ask a single man. He hasn't had his view clouded by experience.   —Milton Newton

Before I got married, I had six theories about bringing up children; now I have six children and no theories.   —John Wilmot, Lord Rochester

──────────────────────────── ■

What Does God Have in Mind for Us?

Many would have us believe that the man's role in home and state has been set in stone since the beginning of time. That is simply not a biblical view. The story of Scripture is that of a God constantly interacting with his people and making provision for them in whatever circumstance he finds them. In many—maybe most—cases where we find God shaping a new provision for his people, he does so because of their fallenness and refusal to live within the constructs of an earlier provision, but the fact that God provides new plans for us in the midst of our fallenness does not make those new provisions any less the will of God for our lives, nor does it lessen our responsibility to be obedient to God's calling.

What is it that God calls us to do? It seems that the agenda is settled in the first few chapters of Genesis. Within the story of creation, humankind is given two tasks: to "be fruitful and multiply," and to "have dominion over" all the earth. The details of how we are to go about accomplishing these tasks are not immediately presented to us. What is most significant about the two assignments given (and also the third task given to us in the New Testament) is that they involve activities most closely associated with the divine activity of God.

When we think of God acting, what are the primary actions that come to mind? We usually think of God as Creator and as Lord over creation. Now look at our assignment. What are we first called upon to do? To be fruitful and multiply. In other words, to create. To join with God in his primary activity, creation of new life, is his very first command to us. Thus, the activity of family, of creating life and sustaining it, is to be part and parcel of our existence.

Then, we are to have dominion. In other words, to rule. The word here translated "dominion" is used throughout the Old Testament to denote the lordship of God, and its Greek corollary in the New Testament denotes the lordship of Christ. It is a term always associated with royal ruling. But here God is, in the very opening of his revelation to us, suggesting to us—no, commanding us—that we are to have the same type of right as rulers of his creation.

There are, to be sure, qualifiers about how we are to exercise this dominion; we will get to that when we talk about stewardship. But, those qualifiers do not lessen the impact of the fact that God desires to share the right of dominion with us. In the context of Genesis, it is clearly a command that we are to responsibly utilize God's creation.

Do you catch what is important about all of this? This sets the agenda for everything we do, because God's commission for us is his statement of how he wants to relate to us. God says he wants to share creation and lordship—the two central acts of Godhood—with us. In those very first words of his revelation of himself to us, God forms a divine/human partnership to accomplish his purpose in the world. We complete the first part of the task in our families. The activity of business, commerce, and productive activity, *responsibly* conducted, is the contemporary expression of the second part of this ancient command.

The Three Principal Demands upon Our Lives

The Command		The Fulfillment		The Arena
Be fruitful	»	The creation of new life	»	The home
Have dominion	»	Responsible stewardship/management of resources	»	The workplace
Be stewards of grace	»	Witness to the truth of the gospel	»	The world

---

And then look what happens when we receive the news of his final activity in the New Testament. As soon as God makes provision for his ultimate redeeming activity in Jesus Christ, he commissions us to participate with him in bringing redemption to his creation. Paul says in Ephesians, "I have been made a steward of God's grace." This is a statement that while salvation is truly a matter of God's grace, he involves us in delivery of that grace through evangelistic proclamation. In whatever he deems to be his most important activities, God always calls us to be partners in participation with him.

Then especially in the activities of family (creation) and livelihood (dominion), we are most about doing the tasks of Christian life. Because both are divine commands, there is no natural conflict between the two; they are the complementary facets of our divine commission. Our work at both is faithful stewardship of the gift that God has chosen to share with us. The tension between the two parts of our task happens only when we allow that task to become corrupted.

Unfortunately, corruption of the divine gift seems to be our history. Sexual immorality (the corruption of the gift of creation) and abuse of power (the corruption of the gift of dominion) pervade our culture. Yet, we do not measure these corruptions evenly. Too often, a double standard is evident in the response of the church. We as Christians are quick to condemn illicit sex but accept and participate in unjust power relationships and structures in our homes, communities, businesses, and even our churches.

But the call of Scripture is to be faithful to God in all that we do. The obligation to refuse the seductive allure of power is no less a command of God than is the call for sexual purity. But the play of power has become an accepted immorality in our culture. Adultery and promiscuity exact their penalty from the spiritual health of both the individual and the community. But, abuse of the gift of dominion is no less injurious and may be even more prevalent. The Giver demands accountability from the recipient.

If we understand the biblical story, however, it must inform us that God has a purpose for us in each task that he gives us. We are not free to corrupt the divine gift. Instead, God shares his divine prerogative with us for two reasons: to form relationships and to model for the world what God intends for these relationships. No less than in the family, our public relationships, whether in the business community, among friends, or even in tertiary contacts, must be reflective of the divine intent. Many men recognize the responsibility to cultivate relationships within their families in ways that help the family members mature and become productive members of the family of God. Too often, however, those same men recognize no obligation to their relationships in the marketplace, even though both sets of obligations spring from the same biblical source.

At the same time, many men have sacrificed their families on the altar of the dollar. Again, this grows from a corruption

■ ───

Managing Both Sides

Don Elliott is certainly the best automobile dealer I've ever met. Located in a small community about an hour's drive from Houston, Texas, Don's dealerships set the kind of sales pace that most urban dealers only dream of reaching. I wouldn't think of buying a car from anyone else. What I like about Don is his integrity and consistency—two words that most folks don't associate with car dealers. But they do with Don.

Don doesn't put on his salesman's persona when he walks into the dealership on Monday morning. What the customer sees of Don is what his family and friends see. "I think who you are comes through in whatever it is you do. The things that make a good businessman are the same things that make a good husband, father, and friend. If you try to be one thing in one place and something else in another, people will recognize the dishonesty."

─── ■

of the stewardship which God has given us. When our vocation begins to be all about money, or power, or influence, instead of about service to God, then things are out of balance.

This improper weighing is not sanctified by the nature of the business. We have all seen those who have lost their families because they were consumed by the power of the pulpit. It is as wrong for the pastor as it is for the salesman. Every business holds within it the potential for great service to God as well as the power to corrupt. It is our task, as men of God, to model for the world the divine intent that both family and vocation be acts of ministry.

Then What Does It Mean to Be Dad?

Within the context of fulfilling the purposes of God, however, we are given tremendous freedom to work out our divinely assigned tasks. Contemporary prophets who present us with cut-and-dried models of what our families or our workdays are supposed to look like completely miss the point. Life with God here in this world is supposed to be a journey, a grand experiment if you will, replete with unexpected events, new conditions, and changes of course. And God is a fellow traveler with us, always providing the means to address the diverse conditions which are the very essence of our existence.

What does God want from us? The same thing that any parent wants from children. He wants us to grow up, to be able to make decisions on our own while never departing from the foundation of our relationship with him. That means that he gives us freedom of choice within the context of tasks. Your family may not look like mine; my understanding of what it means to be a father may be vastly different from yours, but God equips each of us to go about the business of family and the business of business in our own way. And the world is a richer place, more reflective of the God who is our Creator, because of that diversity.

And so each of us is called upon to carve out our own way of being responsible before God. There are, or course, certain restrictions and strictures which guide us within our journey to faithfulness. But those who seek God's will with integrity, faithfulness, and diligence will no doubt find that he is there, guiding, empowering, and comforting. He is forever a willing companion in the journey.

ANSWERING THE CALL

3

Work is the rent you pay for a room you occupy
on earth.
Elizabeth II, Queen of England

That we live in a world of entitlement is no
new revelation. Down through the years, folks have always
seemed to think that position in life is more a function of a last
name than it is of accomplishment. In *Harrap's Book of Business
Anecdotes,* Peter Hay relates the story from the twentieth century's first decades of a letter of recommendation a Chicago bank
received from a Boston investment firm concerning a prospec-
tive employee. The Boston firm, while never mentioning the
young man's work qualifications, did note that his mother was
a Lowell and his father was a Cabot. It also mentioned that he
was related to the Peabodys, the Appletons, and the Saltonstals,
the height of Bostonian aristocracy.

The Chicago firm quickly responded to the Boston firm,
thanking them for the letter of recommendation. But, as they
noted, the recommendation letter really missed the point. After
all, "We are not contemplating using the young man for breed-
ing purposes."

Well said. There is no entitlement in a name nor in position.
Can somebody please explain to me why it is that so many

people genuinely believe that the world owes them something? It is probably because our society breeds that viewpoint. Instead of a world in which each individual takes responsibility for his own actions, an attitude of blaming others and avoiding responsibility permeates not only the workplace, but all areas of life.

Over the last decade, we have witnessed the victimization of America. Everyone, it seems, is a victim. We look at our courts, and we find that the fastest way to win freedom in our criminal justice system is to claim non-responsibility because of previous victimization. Most social programs seem to be based upon the precept that a large segment of the American population has been victimized by society and is, therefore, not responsible for their own well-being. Sometimes that is a valid premise—we must be forever vigilant to protect those, like children, who are unable to protect themselves. At the same time, many of today's "victims" are those who chose not to exercise responsibility.

And it is not a problem limited to the poorer classes of America. We see growing numbers of the white-collar unemployed who claim victimization by a downsizing economy. Their victim status means they do not have to accept the blue-collar job that would put bread on the table but which might damage a precious ego. In America, we have reached a *crisis of responsibility.*

In Chapter 2, we talked briefly about the genesis of the concept of the worthiness of work. In this chapter we want to go a bit beyond that definition. Many scriptural narratives are stories of God calling people to a specific task. Over the next few pages, let's look at work in the context of *responsibility toward the calling of God to vocation.*

Vocation and Calling in Scripture

The words of Scripture comprise a story, and within them we find the narrative of a people who are called into partnership with God for his redemptive purposes. The first explicit calling recorded in Scripture is God's summons of Abram to move out of Haran and to form the beginning of a covenant community. Abram's response to that calling of God was a seminal event in human history, for Abram became the first man to have an explicit sense of vocation. He was about doing God's will by doing God's work in the world.

■ ───

And as He passed by, He saw Levi the son of Alphaeus sitting at the tax office, and said to him, "Follow Me." And he arose and followed Him.
                                                    —Mark 2:14

─── ■

Throughout Scripture, this concept of calling continues to play an important role. Very early in their history, the people of Israel were called as a nation to be a royal priesthood. As such, they had a sense of being agents of divine providence in the world. By the time we reach the New Testament, the concept of calling is an integral part of describing the relationship between God and the believer. Christians are called into God's kingdom (1 Thess. 2:12), to eternal life (1 Tim. 6:12), into light (1 Peter 2:9), into the peace of Christ (Col. 3:15), to an eternal inheritance (Heb. 9:15), to fellowship (1 Cor. 1:9), to freedom (Gal. 5:13), and to holiness (1 Thess. 4:7). Indeed, the very concept of the church is that of a "called-out assembly," seeing themselves, both as individuals and as a collective body, separated for the purposes of God.

According to the apostle Paul, especially, the refusal to respond to the call of God was the mark of immaturity. In Corinthians and Ephesians, he chides Christians for refusing to mature in the faith. But then, on a very positive note, he encourages believers in the fourth chapter of Ephesians to "live a life worthy of the calling you have received" (NIV). He goes on to describe what that means. The believers are to "no longer be infants tossed back and forth by waves." Instead, each one is to take the task that he has been assigned, whether it is to be an apostle, prophet, evangelist, pastor, teacher, or whatever the assignment God has given, so that the whole body grows up into maturity. In other words, within the context of the calling to vocation, Christians are to take responsibility for becoming mature and productive members of the community of faith.

In Scripture, it seems that the concept of calling refers explicitly to a divine commission and to the accomplishment of a spiritual task. The idea of vocation was not applied to a person's occupation, but it in no way denigrated that which was not immediately related to the service of God.

Unfortunately, religious vocation grew to be seen as more "godly" than worldly occupations. During the early centuries of the church, then, a concept of two realms developed: the holy, pious world of the church, and the profane, secular world. Medieval Catholicism saw the concept of vocation only as a calling to religious life with its concomitant obligation to separate from the profane world of the natural order.

A Christian is perfectly free, lord of all, subject to none. A Christian is a perfectly dutiful servant of all, subject to all. —Martin Luther

The idea of work as a vocation or a divine commission comes from the Reformation where it was first developed by Martin Luther and then advocated by John Calvin. As Luther's understanding of justification by faith developed into the doctrine of the priesthood of all believers, it meant that there could be no distinction between a priestly realm and a secular realm. All believers were called to participate in divine vocation. Therefore, there could be no distinction between work in the church and work in the community. All was of God.

Calvin's understanding of sanctification as a process by which the believer continually struggles to become more God-like was a natural home for an understanding of work as vocation. Calvin saw a redeeming struggle in work and individual responsibility within a system of commerce and enterprise.

The calling to vocation in this sense does not refer to a specific setting aside of an individual for a specific task, although many believers can affirm that they have taken a task in life because of divine guidance. Rather, the call to vocation, as understood by Luther and Calvin, is a call to be responsible and productive members of the community, sharing with all others the task of dominion. There is no concept more biblical than that.

Toward an Ethic of Responsibility

The writer Samuel Johnson was almost consumed by his sense of responsibility to be an effective and productive member of his community. As a constant reminder, he posted the words of John 9:4, "I must work the works of him that sent me, while it is day: the night cometh, when no man can work," across the face of his watch (KJV). Always aware of the magnitude of his gifts and talents, Johnson felt he could never measure up to that which was required of him by the gifts he had received, no matter how much he produced. The great output of his lifetime is by and large a product of his drive to answer responsibly for what he had been given.

God will not look you over for medals, degrees, or diplomas, but for scars. —Elbert Hubbard

Conversely, today we live in the midst of a responsibility crisis. When was the last time you heard someone use the word responsibility, except to deny it? In attempting to make a fail-safe society, we have instead developed an all-fail culture. Indeed, the language of nonresponsibility has become the law of the land: diminished capacity, no-fault divorce.

What families and corporations in this society need is a good healthy dose of Christian responsibility. The statement of the young Jesus, "I must be about my Father's business," should be a clarion call to each one of us to get serious about work. Think of the impact that it would have upon our world if each one of us were to make the determination that we would hold ourselves genuinely accountable before God for the actions of our lives. Think of the impact it would have upon your corporation if each employee said, "I'm going to take responsibility not only to do my job as a calling of God, but also to see that this company does its best to be a redemptive force in the community." The whole concept of vocation is based in the idea that as individuals created in the image of God, we are free moral agents, responsible for our actions before a just and loving God. We have had the freedom part down all along; it is probably time we learned to handle the part about responsibility.

Called, Not Driven

Unfortunately, however, an awareness of vocation can easily be perverted into an attitude of drivenness. If we genuinely have a sense that God is working in our lives and using us for a specific task, it is very easy for that task to become all-consuming.

Evidence of possession by a task is apparent in the lives of many executives. The man who always puts the ultimate priority on his work shows such consumption. The executive who micromanages every detail, refusing to delegate responsibility because he feels that no one can do the job as well as he can, gives evidence of the same. The man who is possessed by his vocation often will not brook any opposing opinion about how business should be conducted because he feels that he alone is in possession of the calling.

The Scripture is very clear that our tasks—*even divinely-commissioned tasks*—are never ends unto themselves. Instead, they are the means by which to reach an objective, and that objective is always righteousness. All of the tasks of this earth, no matter what they might be, are to fit within the big picture of leading people to right relationship with God.

Occasionally, it becomes apparent how an assigned task fits into the larger objective of redemption. Take, for example, the job of evangelist. It's easy to see that leading people into a saving relationship with Jesus Christ is a part of God's redemptive plan for this world.

In other situations, it is much more difficult to see how the task can be drawn into the bigger picture. If we look at the short-term objective, for example, it's hard to see how a builder erecting a building can help people become more righteous. If, however, we look at the bigger picture and understand that even erecting a building is a valid expression of the divine commission to have dominion and to be productive, then we can be sure that God is using us to fulfill his divine plan.

Let's talk about maintaining the proper perspective concerning vocation and call. Our guide through these pages will be the life of John the Baptist. Along the way, we will look for those specific characteristics which mark the healthy attitude toward what we will refer to as "calledness."

The story of John the Baptist is one of the most familiar in the New Testament. He was the son of Elizabeth and Zacharias and a cousin of Jesus himself. We first hear of John in the context of the announcement by the angel to Zacharias that a son would be born to him and Elizabeth. After his birth, however, John and his family disappear from public record until the beginning of his ministry.

When he appears again, we find him in the wilderness. There he proclaimed the coming of the Day of the Lord. He called not only the obvious sinners, but also the religious elite of his day to repentance. His prophetic ministry was the preparation for the coming of the Messiah. It is that ministry which sets the guidepost for a measure of understanding of what it means to be called to vocation.

Those who are called have a sense of mission. John's sense of mission freed him to speak with a prophetic voice to the power elite of his day. He told the Scribes and the Pharisees that, just as surely as did the Gentiles and pagans of the region, they needed to repent and then be baptized as a symbol of their repentance. By the time John the Baptist comes back into our view in the New Testament, he has already delivered that message; his ministry has already seen its peak. It is on its way down, and the crowds are leaving him. But because John had a sense of his mission, he was able to understand that his role was by and large completed.

When the news was brought to John that the crowds which had followed him, and even some of his closest followers had become followers of Jesus, one would expect a reaction of jealousy. Instead we find John saying, "You yourselves bear me witness, that I said, 'I am not the Christ,' but, 'I have been sent before Him.'" He understood that his mission was one of preparation. Therefore, as he completed his task, he was willing to give up his position of power.

Those who are called have a sense of identity. We are all familiar with the David Koreshes of this world—those who have genuinely lost touch with reality and tried to assume an identity that did not belong to them. Just as deadly, though, for the purposes of the gospel, are those who have determined that their place in the kingdom is so exalted that they deserve the accolades of lordship right alongside Christ. We have all seen those pastors who proclaim from the pulpit that they are more interested in followship than fellowship, those corporate executives who use their positions of authority to tyrannize their workers, or those leaders so intoxicated by their own might that they sexually exploit those who are victims of their power.

Those who have studied interpersonal communications tell us that it is very easy to confuse the message with the messenger. That is why, in the Old Testament, the people so often turned upon the prophets who brought the word of God's impending judgment. In contemporary society, the problem is not so often that the hearers of the message misunderstand the identity of the messenger, but that the messengers themselves misunderstand who they are. That is exactly what happened at the church in Corinth. The people took such great pride in the spiritual gifts that God had given them that they began to try to claim spiritual authority over one another. They mistook what they had been given with who they were.

That is also why retirement parties seem to be so hard for many people. Retirement should be a celebration of a new beginning, a time of moving into a new arena in life. It should be preparation for a new stage of ministry in life. Instead, for a great number of people, retirement means the end of productive contribution and, therefore, the end of life itself. Because they cannot separate who they are from what they are doing, it virtually means the loss of identity.

In the life of John the Baptist, we find a model of identity worthy of emulation. John understood the difference between the message that he brought and the person that he was. Early on in his ministry, it seems, John had access to a great deal of power. The religious people of Jerusalem and the surrounding area began to come out into the wilderness to hear him preach. To a great extent, he began to replace the religious hierarchy as the voice for the faithful in Israel. Indeed, many began to ask him if he were not the Messiah.

How tempting the call to power must have been. How easy it would have been for John to go along with what were, after all, the judgments of others about his ministry. The temptation to succumb to the intoxication of power must have been almost overwhelming.

But, what we find in John's life is that he understood precisely who he was. He repeats to the crowd, "I am not the Christ." He never lets his commission absorb his identity.

There is only one way that John could refuse the crowds or that we as Christians today can maintain a sense of identity when power beckons us. Only the individual who has a clear sense of being called by God and has an awareness of position in the world can withstand the temptations of power. If priorities are misplaced, if an ego is out of check, or if we are insecure in our identity, then we are easy prey for the temptation of might. The only defense from its onslaught is to live each day in constant communication and dependence upon the God who calls us. In such obedience is protection found.

Those who are called have a sense of stewardship. I sat across the table from the owner of a company. "I am this business," he said. "It exists because, through, and from me. If I'm not here, this company is not here." So much for stewardship. We live in a possessive world, a world where success is measured by how much we own or how much we control.

I once read the resume of a successful pastor. Amidst a recitation of achievements, the job summary boasted that while this man had been pastor of a certain church, "He built its membership from 200 to over 2,000 members." *He did?*

I'm sorry, but the biblical concepts of dominion and stewardship give no room for such possessiveness. The whole idea of stewardship is that we are managing something by divine commission. The moment that "I" or "my" are factored in, the concept of stewardship goes right out the window, and we have lost that sense—and the power—of divine commission.

John the Baptist knew that neither the message nor the crowds belonged to him. Instead, he held them in trust until the coming of the Messiah. His calling was "to make straight the path of the Lord." Therefore, when the crowds began to go over to Jesus, there was no loss for John the Baptist. The crowds had never belonged to him in the first place. The movement only meant that he had done his job. When Jesus became the focus of Messianic hope in Israel, John had not lost his commission; he had fulfilled his mission.

When we as believers understand that we have been given a job, we are able to successfully move away from possession of that task. We are also successfully able to avoid being *possessed by the task,* and that may be just as important. Too many men have been captured by their work. The man who cannot walk away from his office to spend time with his family does not have a sense of stewardship. The corporate executive who cannot let go of any aspect of his work because "No one else can do it as well as I can," does not have a sense of stewardship. Even the father who will not allow a dissenting opinion in his own home has lost the sense of stewardship.

When we have a sense of stewardship, we understand that God has entrusted certain tasks to us. We also understand that in so doing God has made a statement of faith in us, in our abilities and in our worthiness to relate to him. God did not give us the task because we are perfect, but he commissioned us in the midst of our fallenness. What he expects from us is not perfection but faithful management until he directs that management policy or personnel be changed. The called person with a sense of stewardship always awaits further direction from God—and recognizes that God can use anyone he so chooses to deliver that direction.

Those people who are called have a sense of the big picture—and their place in it. I have a good friend who absolutely immerses himself in his work. Whatever project, task, or assignment he tackles becomes of ultimate importance to him. I guess that's admirable—in one sense. It is good that someone can have a sense of focus, of tuning into a job. By so doing, a great deal can be accomplished. At the same time, however, when a person becomes so consumed by a task that it becomes the end unto itself, that the concerns, needs, and tasks of others are forced to become secondary, then something is quite out of balance. The big picture has disappeared.

It seems that John the Baptist had a very clear understanding of the big picture. From the beginning of Jesus' rise to preeminence, John understood that his task was declining in importance: "He must increase, but I must decrease." In John 3:28–29, John the Baptist was quick to point out that, on the larger scale of things, he was not the focus: "You yourselves bear me witness, that I said, 'I am not the Christ,' but, 'I have been sent before Him.' He who has the bride is the bridegroom; but the friend of the bridegroom, who stands and hears him, rejoices greatly because of the bridegroom's voice. Therefore this joy of mine is fulfilled."

John's view of the big picture helped keep him on the track. It must have been tempting, as a prophet in the desert, to use his popularity before the crowds to build an even greater ministry for himself. But, because he understood that, in the big picture, it was most important that Jesus be recognized as the Messiah who would bring salvation to Israel, John did not continue to cultivate the crowds. Instead, he made his ministry subservient to God's greater purpose.

In a like manner, there are few things that we can do in our lives that are more important than catching a glimpse of the big picture. God has a redemptive plan for this world, and he intends for us to be a part of it. If what we do is an end unto itself—whether that end is building a bigger company, making more money, or gaining more personal power—then the temptation to succumb to the allure of Satan can be almost overwhelming. We can use unscrupulous practices to top the competition; we can devote so much time to the completion of what we see as our primary task that we forget all about the relationships that God has given us to maintain; we can push our employees beyond morally acceptable limits. We can—and will—do those things and many more if our work becomes the ultimate answer for us.

If, however, we understand that what we do is a part of God's ultimate plan for this world, then our priorities will be maintained in good form. We will recognize that obedience to

God is the most important thing in life. We are on his agenda rather than our own.

One of the most disturbing stories in all of Scripture is the story of the return of the Ark of the Covenant to the kingdom of David. David had sent a man named Uzzah and his sons to return the Ark of the Covenant to Israel. For transporting the Ark, there was but one command from God: under no circumstance were the people of Israel to touch the Ark itself.

By means of two long poles, the Ark was set on an ox cart to be brought back to Israel. Near the completion of the journey, the oxen stumbled, and the cart began to tip. Wanting to preserve the Ark, Uzzah reached up to steady it—and God struck him dead.

Wait a minute. Wasn't Uzzah doing what was right, trying to preserve the Ark of the Covenant? Wasn't that his task, to bring it in? It certainly seems so. But, remember, God had given but one command, and that was that the people of Israel were not to touch the Ark under any circumstance. If the bigger picture had been seen—that obedience to God was even more important than the preservation of the Ark—then perhaps this tragedy would have never occurred. As it was, Uzzah decided that what he was doing was of such supreme importance that the command of God could be overridden—and it cost him his life.

In this day and time, it is so hard to see a big picture, to understand that God really is working his redemptive purposes in this world. We get so caught up in the immediate battles we must fight that we lose sight of the ultimate victory that God promises. Faithfulness to God begins when we understand that whatever task we have been assigned is simply part of God's larger drawing for all of the world.

I do not know all that it means to be called. Quite honestly, I get very uncomfortable with folks who talk about hearing God's voice or even knowing that they are doing exactly the task that God has planned for them. It's never been quite that clear in my life. I honestly and earnestly seek God, and I am constantly aware of the touch of his hand upon me. At the same time, however, the directions are not always clearly seen, and I am left to seek, with the wisdom and intelligence that he has given me, the best answers that I have each day.

You may never hear the voice of God directing you to your appointment. You may never see handwriting on the wall telling you which job to take or where to live. Lack of sight and sound, however, should never lessen your sense of calling. Being called is less about hearing the voice of God than it is about wisely and righteously utilizing the opportunities he places before us.

In the play *A Man Called Peter,* there is a scene where the young Scotsman is returning home through a fog and hears his name called. He stops to listen. After pausing for a moment, he starts forward again and stumbles and falls. As he's lying on the ground, he reaches forward and discovers that he has missed, by only inches, tumbling into an abandoned quarry. This incident was portrayed as the time when God saved Peter Marshall and channeled his life into Christian ministry.

Throughout the Old and New Testaments, we see very specific incidents of divine calling in a supernatural sense. Moses at the burning bush and Saul on the road to Damascus are the two occasions that stand out most in my mind. I have never seen a bush burning without being consumed, although I have longed to have God speak to me in that way. Neither have I been blinded by a light from above, and I do not think it is just a matter of my own spiritual insensitivity. God has simply never chosen to visit me in that way.

At the same time, however, I have a quiet sense of confidence in the tasks that I am undertaking. I believe that assurance is evidence of divine blessing upon those tasks. To be sure, any subjective feeling can be the devil's tool as well, and we must be forever diligent that we do not delude ourselves into thinking that we are doing right when we are actually about Satan's business. But the ministry of God in our lives should allow us to openly and honestly examine those things we do, and to ask if we genuinely are seeking the will of God.

You may have never stood in a pulpit nor proclaimed the gospel before a group of people. You may have never traveled to an impoverished village in Mexico or brought the Word of God to a pagan outpost. Nonetheless, God calls you to faithfulness, to be a faithful steward and minister within the context of the big picture of his working in your life. This is a call to which we all must respond.

And one last word: Being called doesn't always make it easy. Even John the Baptist had to come back and ask if Jesus really was the Christ. But he remained faithful—and it cost him his life.

Employees in the Image of God

CARLOS CANTU
President and CEO,
The ServiceMaster Company

W hen you pick up the annual report of The Service-Master Company, it is apparent that this is a different kind of business. It's not just that the company's employees grace the cover of the report—many corporations use that approach. It is the obvious range of services that these employees represent. On this cover page we find exterminators, food service providers, maids, lawn care professionals, healthcare providers; the list could go on and on. And each of the divisions of ServiceMaster focuses on the provision of service through these men and women.

You may not recognize the name ServiceMaster, but you have almost certainly seen their service providers: Chemlawn, Merry Maids, Terminix, American Home Shield, or one of the many forms of their Education, Healthcare, or Industrial/Commercial Management Services. ServiceMaster provides consumer services to over 4.5 million homeowners and 500,000 commercial customers through its divisions. Supportive management services are provided to 2,300 healthcare, education, and commercial customers. The company has achieved increased revenues and profits for twenty-three consecutive years, and has had twenty years of total return to shareholders in excess of 20 percent.

Carlos Cantu, President and CEO, has established an atmosphere conducive not only to growth and profitability for the corporation, but also for the employees who make up ServiceMaster. Cantu is very adamant that ServiceMaster has been and will continue to be an inclusive organization. The company's principles formally recognize that diversity—racial, creedal, religious—is a corporate strength. Diversity means recognizing that, in the words of Cantu, "every person is created in the image of God. It also means that each person can contribute and that a unified whole is made possible only by bringing the pieces together with a common mission and goal."

Diversity does not mean, however, that "anything goes." "We have a set of standards and ethical values that are specific," Cantu relates. "We must recognize that effective management of diversity means managing a workforce of individuals. Even though managing people who are different may be considerably more complex than working with people who share the same perspectives, we cannot allow any individual to become disillusioned or frustrated because of a lack of understanding, support, or general sensitivity."

Among its corporate objectives, the first two are the company's focus, and in fact, are two sides of the same coin: *To honor God in all we do,* and *To help people develop.* In visiting with Cantu, it became clear that these goals are not idle boardroom musing. The company puts a great deal of its resources into internal personal development. "Before we ask them to do something, we help them to be something."

With 31,000 employees, helping them to "be something" becomes quite an undertaking. "We want to provide people with the resources to look at themselves and improve themselves," Cantu states. He continues, "When we bring new people on board, we are, in a sense, assigning them dignity by providing them the opportunity to develop." But doesn't that assume a desire for self-improvement on the part of the employees? Cantu affirms that it certainly does. That is why "We look to hire individuals who are willing to take responsibility for perfection."

If all this language about respecting persons as created in the image of God sounds right out of the New Testament, it should be no surprise. My first contact with the organization came through a colleague who said, "I don't know a lot about the company, but every office I've entered has a Bible on the desk."

AND FORSAKING ALL OTHERS

4

Winston, if I were your wife, I'd put poison in
your cup of tea.
Lady Astor

Madame, if I were your husband, I'd drink it.
Sir Winston Churchill

A few years back, I saw a commercial that
I felt captured the essence of business. In this particular advertisement for a major airline, the head of the company had called
all of the executive sales staff into a conference room. He related
that he had just received a call from an old customer who was
canceling his business contract. When he asked the customer
why, he explained to the sales staff, the customer told him that
the company was no longer responsive to his needs, that they
didn't hear what he had to say.

The executive looked at the sales staff and said something
along the lines of "I think the problem is we've gotten lazy.
We've taken to doing all of our business by phone. We don't
even know our customers anymore." With that, his secretary
walked into the room and handed him a packet of airline tickets,
and he began handing them out one by one to his staff as he

recited the cities where each one of them would be going. A saleswoman then asked from the back of the room, "And where will you be going?" He turned and looked at the camera and said, "To see an old friend."

What a great commercial. Not only did the airline get a plug, but we were all reminded that the essence of business is relationships. Long-term success for any corporation is based on the loyalty and the trust of customers which only come through well-developed and well-maintained relationships. The wise executive recognizes this fact and structures the business in such a way that the sales and executive staff interact with clients, with each other, and with the production and administrative staff. Calvin Coolidge notwithstanding, the business of business is relationships. A good part of every executive's day is dedicated to their cultivation.

At Home with Corporate Objectives

To honor God in all we do
To help people develop
To pursue excellence
To grow profitably

The corporate objectives of ServiceMaster stand against a background comprised of two puzzle pieces. The puzzle pieces represent the unique contribution of the individual players unified by a common mission and goal. How many families as carefully articulate a family objective? How many of us recognize the unique assets each member brings to the rites of family? We would not think of doing business without a mission statement. A statement of purpose might help keep our marriages heading in the right direction as well.

If developing customer relationships is worthwhile, how much more so should we be committed to working at the primary human relationships in our life—those of the home? No doubt about it, the maintenance of a marriage in this day and time is difficult. Statistics suggest that even in the very best of circumstances, marriages end up only about an even bet for survival. When the added burden of a husband who travels, or who spends late nights at the office, or who faces constant pressure on the job is factored into the equation, only a very sound relationship can survive the challenge.

In many wedding ceremonies, the minister introduces the concept of marriage by noting that the family is the first institution ordained by God. When we read the initial chapters of Genesis, we are presented with a superb recitation of relationships: between God and the first man, and between the first man and the rest of creation. But when God looks at creation and pronounces it good, he also pronounces that something is missing. The capstone relationship which was to reflect the relationship between God and man was not yet instituted. Scripture records that from the side of Adam God created woman, and after the act of creation, formed a bond between man and woman that preceded and was to supersede all subsequent relationships save that between man and God. Creation was only fulfilled when Adam entered into a relationship with another human being.

■

Until Eve arrived, this was a man's world.
—Richard Armour

■

As the story of creation continues to develop in those initial chapters of Genesis, God shares with mankind a very special task: the creation of new life. I think it is very important to note that the creation of new life can only occur within the context of relationship. Even in this day and age where promiscuity—and even technology—is allowing that relationship to be less and less involved, it still takes two people to make a new life. It is the intention of God, of course, that the new life is to be created only within the context of the lifelong bond of family. From the beginning, it has been God's plan that the greatest gift given us—the ability to create life—be shared between two human beings. Throughout Scripture, the marriage relationship is portrayed as the pinnacle of all human unions, one that must never be superseded by the misplaced priority of other relationships in our lives.

The primacy of the relationship between husband and wife is no less critical today than it was in the beginning. Over the last few years, we have watched a growing national debate concerning the importance of family values. By and large, the debate has centered upon provision for children, entirely missing the primary and foundational step: the health of the relationship between husband and wife. That relationship serves as the basis for all others in society. The basic premise of this debate has been that the nation can only regain its moral strength when its children are healthy, but the health of children is largely a product of a solid relationship with father and mother in the same home.

Ultimately, however, it is not enough for our children to have positive relationships with mother and father. The mother and father themselves must have sound relationships with each other. If they do not, not only will the emotional health of our children be affected, but the community, the church, and even the corporate environment will be affected by the weakness of the relationships at home.

Relating Home and Office

Is it true that we must keep our corporate identities and our family identities separate, that we shouldn't take the office home with us? Yes. And no. In a very real sense, work should stay at the office. Except for rare exceptions, family time should remain family time. Nothing alienates children more than to know that as soon as dinner is over, Dad will disappear into the study to complete the paperwork he brought home from the office. The executive who constantly brings work home to be completed in the evenings or early in the morning communicates to his wife that his business identity is more important than his role as husband. That is a message we cannot afford to send.

Neither must the wife be the target of vented frustrations after a difficult day in the corporate world. We're all familiar with the "kick the cat" syndrome: Dad had a bad day at the office, so he yelled at Mom as soon as he got home; Mom took it out on Johnny; Johnny hit Becky; Becky threw a rock at the dog who then chased the cat up the tree. Wouldn't it have been easier if Dad had just kicked the cat and saved everybody else the grief?

Trite, admittedly, but the point is valid. When the wife becomes the target of frustrations brought home from the office, the whole family suffers. This relationship between husband and wife is too important to allow it to be torpedoed by unresolved issues from the workday.

At the same time, however, we do ourselves and our families a disservice when we bifurcate our lives into corporate and personal selves. The split personality formed when we divorce ourselves into two identities will prevent either of the identities from fulfilling its function. Psychologists tell us that healthy personalities and healthy relationships are possible only for those individuals who have successfully integrated all that they are and all that they do into a composite whole. Your work is a part of who you are; so is your home life. Those two aspects of your identity constantly inform and interact with one another. The compartmentalization of a life prevents the development of healthy personalities, the successful fulfillment of relationships, and the resolution of tasks.

At the same time, your wife needs to be a part of who you are, both in the home and on the job. She needs to understand what it is that you do and how you approach your tasks. Bringing her into all of the equations of your life makes her a partner in your endeavors, and nothing is more important for a healthy relationship than a sense of sharedness in task.

In his wonderful book, *Men Are from Mars, Women Are from Venus,* Dr. John Gray has a chapter entitled "Men Go to Their Caves and Women Talk." That title says it all. Men and women

---

Really *Listening*

A few years ago, 3M launched a great print ad campaign. A series of single-panel, cartoon-type drawings focused on a single aspect of 3M's approach to business. The first ad showed a large collection of interlocking wheels. By one small gear was the single word "squeak." The second panel was blank except for a small "psst." The final ad showed a long line of men in business attire. At the back of the line, one man was obviously shouting. The man at the front of the line was turned with a side toward the back and his hand held behind his ear in a listening position. At the base of each panel were three words: "3M hears you."

That's the point. More and more, successful businesses are learning the art of hearing. It's a talent that needs cultivation in our homes as much as in the workplace. Hearing—not just registering the sounds, but understanding what is being communicated—is the foundation of relationships, whether between business and client or husband and wife. Don't our families at least deserve the attention to communication that our customers and business associates receive?

---

do approach relationships differently. After a long day of fighting corporate wars, a husband wants to come home, find a favorite chair, and get lost in ESPN or the *New York Times.* His wife, conversely, who may have been at home all day and whose constant companion has been a three year old instead of other corporate executives, wants at least a little bit of adult conversation. That's what we call a communication gap.

Conversation about the day's activities establishes a partnership in the tasks of family. The exchange of information not only allows your wife to understand what you are doing and feel a part of it, but it also gives her a chance to catch you up on the family's activities and feel that the tasks she performs are as important to the long-term well-being of the family as are the things that you do.

If your wife works, when you hibernate and leave all of the evening household chores to her, it's very clear that you are passing judgment on the value of what she does as compared to the value of what you do. You are, in effect, saying, "Your job is neither as taxing nor as important as mine, therefore you can take care of things at home." Even in this day when a majority of middle- and upper-class women hold jobs outside the home, studies indicate that there has been very little change in the way the tasks of family are divided. Women still do a disproportionate amount of the household chores and remain the prime communicators of family needs. Most men, it seems, welcome the extra income, but they have not shifted gears in the way that it would seem this changing of family roles requires.

The bottom line is this: leave your work at the office, but communicate with your wife. Bring her into the circle of your activities, and your marriage will be the richer for it. When we learn to integrate the various activities of our lives into a cohesive whole, we are much better at all of the tasks we face, and our relationships are fuller and more enriching. The reward of integration is always worth the effort.

Home as Refuge

Even for the executive who is consumed by passion for his work, who cannot wait to get into the office in the morning, work, by definition, is work. American executives are facing pressures in the office at unprecedented levels. A whole new vocabulary of stress-inducing words has entered the American business lexicon: downsizing, Chapter Eleven, leveraged buyout, hostile takeover. Factor those terms in with the ones that have been around for years—quota, sales goals, losses—and you have a formula primed for disaster. Far too many executives make the determination that they will carry that full load themselves. They will bear the brunt of the trouble and face all problems alone.

A few years ago, an executive came into my office, the lines of worry etched across his face. "I've just got to talk to somebody." He then related the tale of a family business that had run a deficit for six straight quarters, going from well over a million dollars in profit and free of debt just two years before to then owing almost two million dollars. He lowered his head into his hands. "I didn't think the Lord put more on a man than he could handle."

"How is your wife handling this?" I asked. He looked up, surprised at the question, then began to explain that he couldn't tell her how the business was going because she would worry too much. Part of the burden of being the breadwinner, it seemed, was that you carried the load by yourself.

■——————————————————————

The supply of good women far exceeds that of the men who deserve them.　　　　　—Robert Graves

══════════════════════════════ ■

He didn't give his wife nearly as much credit as I did. I'm certain she was much stronger than he ever would have believed, and events in the coming years were to bear that out. I was most stricken in the conversation, however, by what a twisted understanding of the marriage relationship my friend had. He never gave his wife the opportunity to be a full partner in the marriage, to stand as an adult free and capable of making choices and joining in decisions that affected both of them. Instead, he climbed out on a limb to do it by himself, and in the big picture, many of his decisions were simply not that sound.

His lament, "I didn't think the Lord put more on a man than he could handle" might have been right on track, but he had missed one of the prime sources for handling stress that God gives us. The words in Genesis, "It is not good for a man to be alone," are a strong statement from our Creator that we are not intended to shoulder the load by ourselves. The specific purpose in Genesis for the creation of woman was so that which was incomplete and unfulfilled as one could find its fulfillment as two.

The corporate executive who makes his wife a full partner, if not in the corporate structure, at least in sharing the trials and triumphs that make up the working world, will find in that relationship a means of communication and sharing the stress of both trial and triumph. In relying on that relationship and making the home a place of refuge, we begin to fulfill the biblical image of the family. In so doing, we bring fulfillment not only to our lives, but also to the lives of our family members. Just as we are there for them, they are there for us.

Mutual Submission

Ask anyone to recount Paul's teaching on the subject of marriage and, more likely than not, they will immediately turn to the passage in Ephesians where Paul states, "Wives, submit to your own husbands." That's probably the best known verse on family relationships in the New Testament. That doesn't seem solely to be a favorite verse for men either. Go to any seminar led by women for women, and you will almost certainly hear a discussion of what it means to be submissive, even if for many of them submission means manipulating the husband in such a way that he will tell his wife to do what she wanted to do in the first place. In wife/husband relationships, submission seems to be the focal word now.

Ask just about anyone, though, a second question: What verse immediately precedes the one where women are told to submit to their husbands? Few will venture an answer; it's possibly the least known verse in the New Testament. Here's what Paul says (speaking to Christians): "Submit to one another" (NIV). Oh. Same word. Stated in the same type phrase. Yet that is not a command that we want to hear, so we pretty much ignore it and turn immediately to the question of husband/wife relationships.

I'm not sure what all it means that a wife is to submit to her husband. It seems that Paul had pretty strong feelings about it; in fact, he felt strongly enough about it that he said not only are wives supposed to submit to their husbands, but all Christians are supposed to submit to each other. But wait. Does that mean that if my wife is a Christian I am supposed to submit to her too—because all Christians are supposed to submit to one another? Apparently.

I have never found a definition of submission with which I am entirely comfortable. Variances and nuances rarely seem to be genuinely conveyed, but I think the closest we can get to an understanding of submission, at least in terms of the husband/wife relationship, involves mutually seeking the best for each other. In other words, I put the needs of my wife above my own. In fact, that is the gist of what Paul goes on to explain in the rest of that chapter in Ephesians. It also means that my wife is going to put my needs ahead of her own, and, again, that seems to be what Paul has to say.

Such is the picture of the balanced Christian family—a family in which husband and wife, both seeking God's will, are concerned not about their own rights but rather about seeking the best for each other. In such an atmosphere and in such a relationship, both will find freedom and refuge just as God intended in those first chapters of Genesis.

MATERIALISM

5

> All plenty which is not my God is poverty to me.
> Augustine

As did millions of other Americans, my family gathered around the television one evening in the late spring of 1994 and watched as former President Richard Nixon was eulogized. It was interesting to see how very different the perspectives of his life were once he was no longer alive. Gone, it seemed, from everyone's memory were the dark days of Watergate, Deep Throat, and *All the President's Men.* Vivid, instead, were the policy triumphs of China, SALT, détente, and the end of the Vietnam conflict.

Most striking to me, however, was not the Kissinger eulogy nor the Graham message. Instead, I found myself most taken by the voices of the Navy choir as the words of the old Quaker hymn wafted through the trees surrounding the Nixon homestead. "'Tis a gift to be simple; 'tis a gift to be free."

Here, at the funeral of one of the most complex individuals the twentieth century has ever seen, was the quintessential twentieth-century paradox: in the midst of the vagaries, difficulties, and complexities of everyday life, it was recognized that our ultimate freedom and joy lie in the ability to find simplicity.

Or, at least, so we say. Yet who of us, at the very moment we protest our yearnings for a simpler time and protest that life is too complicated, is not making that deal, signing that contract, or adding that responsibility which makes our life measurably more complex? We state our need for one thing, yet we continually strive for another, and the two cannot exist together.

> *I am richer than E. H. Harriman. I have all the money I want and he hasn't.* —John Muir

The world of commerce is a world of men who are much more at home with the *Wall Street Journal* than with Thomas à Kempis; with the NYSE than the exchange of grace; with Frequent Flyer bonuses than with spiritual gifts. For those men, this chapter is not a word of chastisement. It is a word of encouragement, a declaration that freedom from materialism is a possibility even in the midst of the most conspicuously consumptive society the world has ever known—and even when we are participants in that consumption.

Balancing Act

One thing is very clear: if we are to be faithful to the commands of Christ, we cannot separate our lives into a public/secular perspective and a private/Christian lifestyle. Indeed, the commands of Christ are very clear that we must take our faith into the marketplace with us. There can be no such thing as a private discipleship. Either the privacy will destroy the discipleship, or the discipleship will destroy the privacy. The terms are mutually exclusive.

For many men, the issue seems to be one of application. That is, the principles of the relationship with Christ are to be directly applied to the relationships of the marketplace. They treat their customers/clients/associates fairly, they deal honestly with all people, and their methodology of doing business is constantly informed by their relationship with Jesus Christ. If you do business in a Christian manner, does that not put the stamp of approval on the business enterprise?

It is important to recognize, however, that there is an issue much more basic than application. Perhaps we can ask the question like this: Is the very business of business possible within the Christian context of anti-materialism so evident in the New Testament?

Can the Bottom Line Be Christian?

When I first came to be employed in higher education, I had what I considered to be some very lofty and noble understandings of the purpose of a university education. I was very much a proponent of knowledge for the sake of knowledge, believing that, by and large, learning should have no end other than itself. But then, a recruiting piece for a university came across my desk for review. Expecting an erudite articulation of the rationale for student scholars, I instead found: the primary purpose of an education was to prepare students to pursue a career which would enable them to fulfill their lifestyle goals. There it was in black and white. Even an academic institution was about producing a product, giving a return on investment, and turning the wheels of commerce.

Almost from its inception, ours has been a world of individual commerce and accumulation and management of wealth. At the same time, however, our history is replete with examples of those who have proven that the pot of gold which we pursue at the end of our own rainbows simply does not bring happiness.

Howard Hughes died a miserable recluse; Malcolm Forbes found no solace in wealth; and yet we still somehow believe that gold brings contentment. For the Christian, there must be a better way.

Dr. Bill Hillis relates a story that really gets to the heart of the matter. In the late 1960s, Dr. Hillis, his wife, and their three children lived in Calcutta, India, where he was a research scientist with the Johns Hopkins Center for Medical Research and Training. They were also members of Carey Church, Calcutta, whose namesake, William Carey, pioneered mission work to the Indian subcontinent.

Calcutta is a vast sea of poverty that confronts all those who live there, no matter their station in life. A group of young people from Carey Church invited the Hillis family to join them for the Feast of Puja, which, although a pagan holiday, nonetheless allowed the Christian community an opportunity to gather for celebration. After a game of cricket in the botanical gardens in Howrah, the young people gathered for the "feast"—a large scoop of rice with a bit of curry sauce served on a banana leaf.

Dr. Hillis relates, "As we sat down on a hillock to eat, out of the corner of my eye I caught a glimpse of the street children with bloated bellies and hollow eyes waiting for us to finish so they could scavenge the scraps. I was struck by the paradox of the starving children waiting for the Christians to finish the feast. I picked up my leaf of rice and took it over to them. At first they ran away, but I motioned them to come back and offered them the rice. My family joined me, and the children virtually pounced on the rice."

What was really striking for Dr. Hillis, though, was the action of the young people of Carey Church who followed his lead. "Giving up this feast did not mean that much to my family because we had plenty of food back at our house. For many of those young people, this really was a feast. For them to give their food up to the children was a real sacrifice. In the twenty-five years since, I have not been able to get over that image of those children."

What kind of difference would it make for each one of us if we were confronted with the stark reality of how most of the world lives? We are called to engage the world, not ignore it in our security.

■

No Easy Answer

It seems that when we examine Scripture, with all its discussion of wealth and the entrapment that wealth can bring, all of the commandments on stewardship and using our wealth for the glory of God's kingdom, and all of the warnings about the dangers of materialism, we Christians would have a better grip on the subject of materialism than we do. There really should be some easy answers. Perhaps someone can supply a list of 1–2–3 rules that will allow us to put everything in its correct place.

In fact, I once heard a sermon by a nationally recognized minister which placed the question of wealth into just such a perspective: a 1–2–3 approach to all of the questions dealing with prosperity in an age of poverty. I was singularly unimpressed. The refuge of the Christian has too often been the simple answer, the refusal to engage with the difficult issues of our day and to recognize that the Christian walk is not always one of quick and easy responses, that sometimes it takes genuine soul searching and an attempt to deal from a position of integrity with questions that have no simple or immediate answers. And yet, that is the task always before us.

And so it is with the issue of materialism. Any person who makes an honest attempt to correctly balance the scales when dealing with the issue of materialism recognizes that the easy answers almost always slip into legalism. It would be very helpful if we could put a dollar amount on what it means to be nonmaterialistic; if we could say that a Christian family of four should keep no more than x amount of dollars with which to meet their physical needs, that our savings account should only reach a certain level, and that only so many square feet per person should be permissible in our home. But that is not the answer either. To lapse into a pharisaic legalism can be as deadening for the spirit as is crass materialism. That simply is not the pathway which Christ laid out for us.

We must also confront the very real fact that many people seek to manipulate God in questions of wealth. The Christian church today is afflicted by those who preach a gospel of health and wealth, encouraging us to tithe, ostensibly to meet the purposes of God's kingdom, but in reality so that God can return that "seed faith" many times, allowing the giver to experience wealth beyond imagination. A perversion, adaptation, and baptism of the American dream of financial success at times seems to permeate the church. Many ministers appear to tell us that God does mean for us all to experience financial success, in spite of all the biblical evidence to the contrary. The poor are not blessed; they are cursed by man and God in much of our contemporary theology. By giving it away (to their ministry, of course), the high priests of the health and wealth gospel claim we are showing God that we can be trusted with the greater financial success with which he will undoubtedly reward us.

Such a caricature of the American dream is anathema to the message of Scripture. Those who buy into the health and wealth gospel are seeking not to serve God; rather, they are investing in the church in a *quid pro quo* in order to line their own pockets and to achieve the wealth to which they think they are entitled.

The New Testament knows nothing of an investment gospel. The call to faith is always presented as a call to take up the cross and be crucified with Christ. Look at the lives of the apostles. If there is a biblical path to material wealth, they never discovered it. Christianity has never been and will never be about material gain. Those who suggest that it is preach a message genuinely satanic in content.

Legalism and seed-faith Christianity are opposite sides of the same coin. Both represent the quick and easy answer to the gospel challenge put forth by Jesus Christ. And both represent attempts to manipulate God, to call upon him to do our bidding rather than genuinely seeking to be obedient to his. For the believer, there must be a better way.

Dependence—A Biblical Perspective

How can we—in a culture absolutely consumed by materialism, in a society in which millions go to bed hungry while others flaunt ostentatious wealth—attempt to be faithful to our Lord's call to be free from materialism? One cannot help but see the overwhelming simplicity of the life of Christ. Even a cursory examination tells us that he was not consumed by the "important" issues of his day. Rather, his focus was on the timeless questions of relationship with God and with other people. How did Jesus, with the same physical needs and desires that drive all of us, manage to escape the clutches of materialism?

Seek simplicity—and distrust it.
—Alfred North Whitehead

Let's look at his life for clues. It seems that the overwhelming characteristic of his life was his trust of God the Father. From the mundane: "Look at the birds of the air, for they neither sow nor reap nor gather into barns; yet your heavenly Father feeds them," to the most profound: the placement of his eternity in the hands of the Father as he prepared for the time of the cross—"Not my will, but thine, be done" (KJV). Then, following shortly thereafter, he makes the statement of ultimate reliance: "Father, into thy hands I commend my spirit" (KJV). Throughout the New Testament, the life that Jesus models is a life of absolute and utter dependence on the Father. And in that dependence, he reveals a freedom that is open to all of us.

One of the great lessons from Jesus' life is in that garden prayer. Notice the two phrases that dominate the prayer. First, he calls upon his relationship with God: *"Abba,* Father." What is telling in this exchange is the reflection of the relationship that is given in Jesus' words. Jesus calls God Father. But Christ does not stop with that plea. The word used is not one of formal address, but one of close relationship. The close intimacy of that call is immediately followed with "not my will, but thine." And in that juxtaposition is the lesson for us: the privilege of calling God Father is always dependent upon the relationship of obedience.

"Stop doing wrong, learn to do right! Seek justice, encourage the oppressed. Defend the cause of the fatherless, plead the case of the widow. Come now, let us reason together," says the LORD. "Though your sins are like scarlet, they shall be as white as snow; though they are red as crimson, they shall be like wool. If you are willing and obedient, you will eat the best from the land."

—Isaiah 1:16b–19 NIV

When we as Christians begin to talk about our relationship with God, the first line of that relationship is dependence, but it is reflected immediately in obedience; understanding the interrelatedness of those two sides of the relationship will lead us to call upon God as our provider and sustainer but will also call us to obedience to him.

In Scripture, the idea of God's provision is seen in the celebration of Jubilee in the Old Testament. In Leviticus 25, the Year of Jubilee was commanded by God as a time of celebration of his generosity and the freedom that such generosity provides for us. Once every fifty years, on the Day of Atonement, the trumpet sounded throughout the land, proclaiming liberty to all its inhabitants. All debts were forgiven, land was reverted to the original property holders, and slaves were set free.

The whole concept of Jubilee was grounded in the bedrock conviction that God would sustain his people and provide for them:

The Principle of Jubilee:
- God will make provision

The Decree of Jubilee:
- All debts forgiven
- All slaves set free
- All land returned to its original owners

The Promise of Jubilee:
- The breaking of a cycle of poverty
- Wealth became temporal and, therefore, not the means to lasting power
- The abolition of a caste society
- The realization that land and wealth did not belong to the people; rather, the people were stewards of what God gave them
- Dependence upon God
- The joy of freedom from financial concerns

There is absolutely no evidence that the Hebrew children ever implemented this divine command. But then, there are many commands they did not follow properly. How differently the history of our world might have been written had this concept of dependence become the foundation for their society. How would we approach our finances today—our relationship to money—if we really saw ourselves as the temporary managers of God's gift, if possessions were not an end to themselves but rather something which we care for in God's behalf? Is such a standard attainable today?

Cheap Grace

One of the great stories of the twentieth century is that of German pastor Dietrich Bonhoeffer. As a young man watching Hitler's rise to power in Germany, Bonhoeffer was offered a prestigious pastorate in the United States. He left his homeland and came here to assume a pulpit ministry. The focus of his theology was what he referred to as the "problem of cheap grace." Cheap grace, according to Bonhoeffer, was that which many Christians sought—all of the benefits of being called Christian without the responsibility or trials. He saw this as a problem permeating the church.

> *Throughout the history of the church, there have been those groups and individuals who took very seriously the instruction to exercise wise stewardship. Clement wrote, "Let everyone be subject to his neighbor . . . let the rich man provide for the wants of the poor; and let the poor man bless God, because He hath given him one by whom his needs may be supplied." No idle words, those: By A.D. 250, Christians in Rome were feeding 1,500 people.*

For Pastor Bonhoeffer, cheap grace was not idle pulpit talk but, instead, something that challenged the very core of his existence. Recognizing the costliness of Christ's sacrifice and the call to each of us to respond in kind, Bonhoeffer returned to his native Germany to be with his people in a time of national trial. By that juncture, Hitler had total control of the reins of power. The German National Church had been totally co-opted by the Nazis. It was no longer the body of Christ; it was the agent of Hitler.

Bonhoeffer and a group of fellow Christians formed what came to be known as the Confessing Church. Bonhoeffer was bold enough to say that the Confessing Church "was the will of God for Germany." But in the midst of doing the will of God, there was no easy path.

The fellowship of the Confessing Church stood in opposition to everything that Hitler's regime preached for Germany. Struggling to discern the Christian response to the evil of Nazism, the young pastor became convinced that Hitler must be stopped at all costs. Because he did not want the church itself to be associated with his actions, he resigned his position in the church and became involved in a plot to assassinate Hitler. The plot failed, and Bonhoeffer and his coconspirators were arrested and sent away to a concentration camp. Only days before the Allied troops liberated the camp, with the guns of the advancing army sounding in the distance, Bonhoeffer was taken from his cell and executed.

Even to those imprisoning him, the young theologian had become "Pastor Bonhoeffer." He was minister to everyone who came into his sphere of contact, be they prisoner or guard, warden or captive. His *Letters from Prison,* a collection of his correspondence written while in captivity, are among the most moving of all Christian devotional literature. Dietrich Bonhoeffer understood the great cost of grace.

We, too, are called upon to abandon cheap grace. The cost of our salvation was expensive for our Savior. It cost him his life. Yet how often do we approach with a transactional Christianity, wanting the *quid pro quo,* wanting to know what's in it for us? Such an attempt to meld the philosophy of egoism and the truth of self-sacrificial Christianity will be forever dangerous to the soul. Yet on every hand, we see Christians who are quite content to be more concerned with the bottom line than with stewardship and dependence.

As it was for Bonhoeffer, we too must be consumed by the question not of "What is in it for me?" but "What may I surrender?" John F. Kennedy's famous inaugural decree, "Ask not what your country can do for you. Ask what you can do for your country," applies more to the kingdom of God than it does to the state of man. To be certain, the issue for us will always be the great cost of discipleship.

What Drives Our Value System: The Answer of Integrity

The two poles of legalism and license forever hang as a threat to genuine freedom from materialism. Throughout the ages, many of those who have attempted in good faith and integrity to formulate an honest response to the question of wealth for Christians in a world dominated by poverty have constructed artificial systems which consisted primarily of prescriptions of what Christians may not do. A Christian *should not* have this much money, *should not* possess this much land, *should not* live at this standard.

Such legalistic attempts invariably fall into an excess which speaks little of the living God's power to shape and transform our lives. Such an approach is not capable of offering us the necessary subtle distinctions which recognize the different conditions in which we live.

■ ─────────────────────────────────

People's wealth and worth are very rarely related.
—Malcolm Forbes

═══════════════════════════════ ■

For example, I have seen formulations which suggest that believers should not allow their incomes to rise above the worldwide average. I'm sorry, but I cannot live up to that standard. Most of the world lives in poverty. While I might choose poverty as an option for myself, I am not at all sure that I have the right to make that choice for my family. I have an obligation to see that their material needs are met, that my daughters receive the nutritional requirements for a healthy childhood, and that they live in an environment that is conducive to their educational needs.

At the same time, my work requires certain standards of dress as well as adequate transportation in order that I might relate to clients and colleagues. Were I to take a vow of strict poverty, I simply could not meet the prerequisites of my job.

For most of us, poverty itself would end up being some sort of self-serving, pious indulgence, an attempt to salve a conscience guilty because we have too much in a world that has so little. At the same time, however, it would be an irresponsible answer, one that refuses to deal with the genuine difficulties of life in this world.

In reality, however, very few of us ever really struggle with the question of poverty. I know it has never tempted me. We are much more likely to look at the "excess" of those who have sought lives of poverty and use that excess as an excuse for our own self-indulgence and wealth. We see the poverty of the monastics—the simple lifestyle, vows of chastity, vows of silence, vows of poverty—and label their lives, possibly correctly, as fanaticism and therefore simply not an alternative for us today.

At the same time, however, how much more excessive are the lifestyles of many of the Christians that we see modeled in church every Sunday? Individuals and families of conspicuous wealth and even more conspicuous consumption seem to have no concern for the impoverished conditions not only of the Third World, which seems far away and remote, but of their own back door and neighborhood. Nor is there recognition of the toll that such wealth exacts from their own souls. At least the monastics were erring on the side of trying to do what was right and trying to be faithful to our Lord's commands. Faithfulness has little to do with those whose excess is on the side of wealth and waste.

Is there a ground in the middle where we can meet, or at least a place where we can stand in integrity? Even to say "I'll go halfway between what I consider wealthy and where the monastics are" lapses into legalism. How can the Christian respond?

Freedom from Rights

We live in a rights-possessed age. Scarcely a day goes by that some new rights group is not formed: men's rights, women's rights, gay rights, animal rights, children's rights. The list goes on and on. But please, let us never hear about Christian rights. One of the greatest gifts that God has given us is the gift to be free from rights.

The very genius of the New Testament ethic is that we surrender our right to be free, that we surrender our right to have our own way, that we even surrender our right of privacy so that we can live in fellowship with God and other believers. The secret of genuine Christian freedom is found in this surrender.

The paradigm for Christian living is found in the great hymn of Philippians 2 in which we are told that Christ gave up his equality with God—the rights of Godhood—and became "obedient to death—even death on a cross!" (NIV). And, as Paul says, we are to "have this same mind" among ourselves. The record that is brought in the New Testament is of individuals who, over and over again, surrender what they had the right to claim for themselves for the good of the body of Christ.

If we begin our daily walk without the preconception of rights, then surrendering to the will of God becomes easier for us. The paths that we are to walk become much more clear. On the other hand, if our lives are a battle about what God owes us and what we should have the freedom to do, then we will be trapped by legalistic line drawing and nit-picking. We will want to be sure that our rights do not get trampled. Freedom itself can become a captor. We will be forever diligent that we get what is rightfully ours.

When getting our fair share becomes the consuming objective, the Christian drops into a rules accounting to make sure that the definitions are so tightly worded that nothing slips through the net. We get lost in the quagmire of legalism. Again, the promise of divine provision—that God will see to it that our rights do not get trampled—makes it easy to forgo our insistence that we are protected. We become free from the concern of self-defense. Our self-esteem is based not upon an inherent quality of inalienable rights, but upon the richness of the divine relationship that God desires to share with us.

In this context, perhaps the first right we need to surrender is our right to view our personal wealth as a strictly private matter. In this day of politically correct language, tabloid television, tell-all tomes, and gossip journalism, subjects once considered intensely personal and, therefore, forbidden for public discourse now seem to dominate our conversations.

One area that we still do not talk about, however, is personal finance. We want everybody to know before the discussion even begins that our money is our business, and how we deal with it is our business, and no one has any right to question what we do with "the money that God has given us."

At one time in the not-too-distant past our ministers felt a certain obligation to raise the question of finance often, and usually quite loudly, from the pulpit. Though we might have been made somewhat uncomfortable by the "tithing sermon," we did understand that the church had a responsibility to instruct us in the discipline of financial stewardship as well as to demand some degree of accountability from us.

Those days are past. Perhaps the health and wealth message of those who claim to be ministers of the gospel of Christ but who are, in reality, little more than religious privateers has soured our view of the church's relationship to our personal finances.

And, indeed, perhaps the church has lost some of its moral authority concerning wealth. Religious country clubs masquerading as places of worship and Christian education somehow seem very inconsistent with the church preaching a gospel of dependence upon Jesus Christ to a child hungry for the love of Christ as well as food for the belly.

The apocryphal story is told of St. Thomas Aquinas finding Pope Innocent IV in the vaults of the Vatican, running his hands through the hoards of wealth that the medieval church had accumulated. Pope Innocent IV looked at the saint and said, "Well, Thomas. No longer can the church say 'silver and gold have I none.'" And Thomas, with the insight of one whose faith is a daily reality, responded, "But neither can we say, 'in the name of Christ, take up your bed and walk.'"

Perhaps the church by its attitudes toward wealth has lost some of its moral authority to speak to the spiritual questions of material possessions. Nonetheless, the damage we do to ourselves by privatizing questions of personal finance is very real. Just as our entering into the community of Christ has called us to forfeit the right to a private morality in such issues as sexual standards and integrity, so does the church have the right to hold us accountable for the way we manage our money. We are free moral agents, to be certain, but we are accountable moral agents.

Specificity Yet Freedom

In the midst of all of the warnings against the danger of legalism, we must nonetheless recognize that we—both individually and corporately—must be specific about what it means to embrace a simple lifestyle in the midst of a materialistic world. Just as we feel a household budget is a necessity, so should we also ask ourselves some hard questions about our lifestyles. Each aspect of the way we live should be examined in the light of both the promise of Scripture (that God will provide all of our needs) and the demand of Scripture (that we are to be faithful stewards for him with all he has given).

It is an enterprise fraught with danger. The threat of legalism, which is that great quencher of the spirit, hangs ever present. Yet such is the risk we must take. For if we do not, license will not be a risk, it will be a reality. Therefore, we enter the process advisedly, knowing full well its central importance to our Christian walk and constantly aware that God provides the way.

What is the difference between legalism and specificity? Simply put, legalism takes the applications of universal principles and tries to make them into law, while specificity gives hard guidelines for living that still recognize and make provision for the individual circumstances of our lives.

Throughout the Old Testament and into the New, there are many practices outlined which would be either unworkable or simply ineffective today. As Richard Foster notes in *Freedom of Simplicity,* the law of gleaning, so beautifully illustrated in the story of Ruth and Boaz, makes very little sense for us today. This practice was given to the children of Israel so that the poor might always have ample food. Farmers were instructed, as they harvested their grain, to leave the corners of the field uncut so that the impoverished could come into the field and gather the remnants of the grain, thereby having provision. What a wonderful, beautiful, and gracious command—for its time.

It would be meaningless today for the Nebraska wheat farmer to make sure that his combines do not catch the corners of his wheat field. Such action would certainly have little effect on the poverty in Chicago. But a legalistic approach to Scripture tells us that's exactly what we should do.

Specificity, conversely, allows us to look at the underlying principle and ask what specific steps we can take in our own lives to meet the biblical edict. The principle from the Old Testament is easy to discern. Since God is the giver of all provision, those who have been entrusted with a large amount have a responsibility to see that those who have received little can access the bounty. With that premise as our guiding context, we then immediately begin to look for concrete steps in our own lives which allow us to begin to meet such needs. Such freedom to act within the constructs of a life situation is the basic superiority of specificity over legalism.

The Answer of Integrity

Remember the old adage that ends ". . . but you can't fool all of the people all of the time"? Far too often, it is ourselves that we deceive. We construct our own little world and our own little paradigms of righteousness, convinced that we are doing the will of God for our time. Yet, when we really examine our lives, we find that, especially when it comes to the freedom from materialism, we fall far short of the biblical standards. Because gleaning would not work today, because a government system offers some protection for poor children, because "the poor are just lazy anyway," we ignore the needs of society around us and continue to live in the way that we most desire.

Such attitudes overlook the basic premise of the Bible's teaching on stewardship. God calls us to be responsible stewards, not because of what that will do for everyone else, but because of what it will do for us. He very well could have chosen to be the sole agent of provision, to be the sole agent of creation and sustenance, and to be the sole agent of redemption. That was within his purview. That he did not do so must mean that he sees it profitable for us to be involved in these activities.

Yes, certainly the poor and needy are damaged when we are irresponsible stewards, but so are we. We fall far short of what God intends for us in relationship, and we can never find the fulfillment that he desires for our lives. What is the answer to all of this? It seems to me that, as in so many areas of our Christian life, the ultimate answer lies in spiritual integrity. Spiritual integrity is the openness and the willingness to examine our lives in light of what God has called us to do and to seek openly and honestly to be faithful to him. This is one of the most difficult endeavors that we can ever take for ourselves *because we are usually the only ones who know whether or not we have been faithful to that task.*

Such integrity means taking a lot of risks. It means, first of all, openness to the Christian community around us. My good friend, Dr. Barry Harvey, constantly reminds me that Christianity takes place within the community. The needs of the community itself call us to a lifestyle of simplicity. To be free from a consuming materialism means that we must hear the voice of that community and be responsive to it.

Integrity also means making the hard choices—about lifestyle, possessions, and possibly even about position in the community beyond the church. Such integrity can cause conflict with family and friends, with people who simply don't understand why we make the choices we make. Yet, if we are faithful to the cause of Christ, answering the call of the gospel is answering in spite of community pressure. Hard choices yes, but choices rooted in the relationship with Jesus Christ.

Finally, integrity means making the conscious choice to live a life dependent upon the provision of God, to genuinely accept his promise not only that he will provide, but also that our true fulfillment as persons will come not through the accumulation of wealth but through learning dependence upon God's actions in our lives. Such recognition is the final step in Christian maturity. It is the moving beyond the place where everything has to be nailed down for us. Surrendering the specifics of our lives today, realizing that the rules may change tomorrow. We must accept that tension as God works in our lives.

To End Up Where?

Where does that leave us? It leaves us practicing germinal, New Testament Christianity and standing in conflict with perhaps the most universal problem the church has ever faced. The story is told of a missionary visiting an indigenous pastor in an impoverished section of Africa. The missionary inquires of the pastor, "And what is the greatest problem your people face?" to which the pastor replies in one word, "Materialism." The missionary looks around, sees parched fields, rib-apparent cattle, and mud hollows. "Materialism!" he exclaims. "In this place?" The native pastor proclaims, "Materialism is less about what you have than it is about what you desire." And so we, too, struggle daily with a problem that is not just a challenge for the wealthy, but one that is faced by all.

I once picked up Richard Foster's *Freedom of Simplicity* hoping for a quick and easy answer to the question of materialism. I found there were no easy answers. It is a difficult process to find a place where we may be free from materialism, but it's a journey worth taking. And it's a journey that shapes and blesses everyone's life. The good news is that we are not facing a new phenomenon; the problem is as old as mankind. And throughout the history of his relationship with man, God has made provision for those willing to forsake materialism and be dependent upon him. It's a battle that can be won and has been won by thousands of individuals who choose to place their faith in God rather than in things. In our day, it very well may be more difficult because of the great affluence available to so many of us. Yet as great as the difficulty, even greater is the grace of God.

Values in the Corporation

ANSEL CONDRAY
Executive Vice President,
Exxon, U.S.A.

The name Exxon is synonymous with big business. For many Americans, big business means the impersonal, the greedy, even the pernicious multinational corporation. The media caricature of the often evil entity is the image that first comes to mind when we think of a company the size of Exxon.

But then you run into a man like Ansel Condray. Ansel is Executive Vice President of Exxon, U.S.A. He is responsible for development and production operations. The Exxon natural gas commercial unit reports to him. He also oversees Exxon Pipeline Company as well as Sea River Maritime, Inc. He has all of the credentials, the position, and the power to fit perfectly the image of the heartless corporate executive.

The only problem is, the first time you talk to Ansel Condray, you get the overwhelming feeling that you've just met an incredibly humble and personable individual. I asked Mr. Condray to address the issue of how a Christian takes his faith to the workplace, not in a Bible-thumping manner, but as that permeating faith that informs all that we do. From the perspective he offered, there are both positive and negative aspects to having faith in the workplace, but, in the end, the negatives really don't seem to be that important—and perhaps they are not negatives at all.

"In the long-term, for the business community, the most important thing is integrity," he suggests. The Christian cannot wear his faith on his sleeve. But when other businesspeople are aware of the depth of your commitment to Christian principles, that commitment cannot do anything but help the way they look at you. Condray suggests that it may be more difficult for the young executive than it is for the one who is already established in his career. "Early on, they feel like they have to do certain things or participate in certain types of social activities in a way that they probably wouldn't if they didn't feel that pressure."

What advice would he give the young executive in that type of situation? "My advice would be twofold. First, in the long term, your Christianity is much more important than your job. If you felt that compromising your faith were necessary, you would probably make the wrong decision anyway. Secondly, I don't believe that in the long term it's necessary to compromise in that manner anyway." Along those lines, he relates a story of his early days at Exxon. As a young executive, he made the conscious decision that he would not drink at social functions. He would attend and participate, but he would not partake of alcohol. "I never called attention to that, but, of course, people around me could observe it." As you might imagine, that can make the situation somewhat awkward for a young executive who was, quite naturally, concerned with the way his superiors looked at him. Then, one day his boss, who was not a teetotaler, came up and remarked to Condray how much he appreciated the stand the young man was taking. "That sort of thing sticks with you."

One of the most important statements that we can make about our faith comes in the way we do our work. "A Christian has an obligation not to be a slacker. The Christian must be reliable, dependable, and put himself into the business of doing a good job. We may not be the most talented, the most skillful, or superior. We are all different, and we do have to play the cards we are dealt, but it is important that we approach our job with the very best that we have."

So often in popular culture, the big corporation is portrayed as the most evil of all institutions. How can a Christian today walk in the world of big business, given the way many people look at a company like Exxon? "One of the things that is most satisfying for me in my career is that the real principles that guide our corporation are so high. We operate on the principle that results are important, but how we get those results is just as important. Never in my career have I been asked to do anything that was illegal, unethical, or even shady.

"Around the world, Exxon provides jobs for 90,000 people. I genuinely feel that our corporation contributes to society both in its product and in the livelihood that we give to so many people. A corporation is just a bunch of people, but other people have a hard time seeing that. We not only provide the jobs and the services; we also contribute to our society through all types of volunteer activities."

If we as Christians can always remember that a corporation is people and that the values we form and the values we take to the marketplace will by and large shape the nature of the corporation, then we can recognize the kind of impact that can be had not only on our office, but on our country and our world.

CAN'T BUY ME LOVE

6

Baby don't care too much for money.
noted relationship counselor P. McCartney

The contrast couldn't have been more stark. As pictures of starving Rwandan children with bloated bellies and vacant eyes came into my home on the evening news, my eleven-year-old sat down on the couch beside me: "Why can't I have my own telephone in my room? A lot of my friends do." What? We're talking about children having their own telephones when millions of children around the world are starving? The first impulse is to lash out strongly, to chastise a child for even thinking about such matters, to ask what's wrong with American youth that they think they have to have everything, right now.

But upon further reflection, was that question really out of line? Was it not a legitimate inquiry for a young girl, someone who really does have an excellent set of values, and many of whose friends do have telephones in their rooms? No, it was a very good question, one that was to have significant impact in our family. We began as a family to look at the question of "How much is enough?" not just on a personal level but on a family level, to ask ourselves what kind of lifestyle was fitting for us as Christians in a consumer society.

In the last chapter, we dealt specifically with the questions of materialism, but we did so from the perspective of making a personal choice. In some ways, the equation becomes much more complex when we factor in our families. It is one thing to say that I will live a simple lifestyle, that I will limit my consumption, that I will take care of meeting the needs of those less fortunate around me. It is quite another thing to say that we as a family will limit our consumption, that perhaps I will not spend as much on my children as I could because there are others who are needy. What father is there among us who does not want to provide the very best (and we too often define that in a material sense) for his children? If it's in another child's toy box, we want our children to have it too. On the first day of school, we want our daughters to have the designer labels on their clothes and our sons to sport the latest name recognition, pumped up, air-cushioned high-tops. Deep down, we may understand that by so doing, we really aren't providing the best for our children, but it's so very hard to say no.

A father is a banker provided by nature.
—French proverb

During the time of my own childhood, I understood quite readily the definition of wealthy. Rich was whoever had more money than we did. My family now resides in the kind of home and lives at a standard that was only available to the "rich kids" of a generation ago. But for my children, wealthy is still that social level one step up from where we are.

Perhaps it is all just a matter of perspective. Wealth always has been and always will be a very relative thing. Ninety-nine percent of the world's population would consider all but the poorest segment of American society to be very wealthy. Our perception has a lot more to do with a desire to accumulate and possess than it does with any absolute standard. Wherever we are, we seem to want just a little bit more. That is not entirely true—some people want a lot more.

Since we dealt extensively in the last chapter with freedom from materialism at a personal level, the operative question here is how we can translate those values that we understand into language that our children can comprehend. Let me suggest that if we are to relate this concept of freedom from materialism to our children, there are three overriding concepts which must be fully integrated into our lives.

1. *Parents must model a life that constantly demonstrates a proper relationship to God's material provision.* This involves all aspects of life. In a very real sense, we lose the moral authority to tell our children no to things that we do not think are good for them if we have no such self-restraint when purchasing for ourselves. If the children see that the family budget is strained each month as Mom and Dad try to pay off the credit cards that have temporarily sated the drive to possess, words about freedom from materialism will certainly ring hollow. Instead, our children will see a lifestyle that consumes at all costs, one that speaks nothing of the enriching and providing hand of God in our life.

It is one thing to praise discipline; it is another to submit to it. —Cervantes

---

This does not mean that our children have to see us in poverty. Some of the most materialistic people that I have encountered also happen to be very poor, yet they remain consumed with the desire to possess. Conversely, some of the people who are most free from materialism have been given stewardship of a great deal by God and use that stewardship to benefit all of those with whom they come into contact. Materialism—and freedom from it—has never been particularly class conscious.

What this does mean, however, is that our children must see a permeating stewardship throughout our lives. It also means that they must be involved in that stewardship. Such an involvement entails a fairly comprehensive education program. Children need to understand the price of things. They need to know how the family's money is budgeted. They need to see how those who are not as fortunate live.

A recent HUD advertisement featured children talking about the possibility of purchasing a home. The children were allowed to venture guesses as to how much a home would cost. Their estimates ran from $500 to $500,000,000. As I watched the commercial, it struck me that very few children have any concept of large amounts of money, of the sacrifices that are necessary to purchase a home and to make daily provision of food and clothing. Very few children have any involvement in the budgeting process of the family.

If our children are to understand the concept of stewardship and understand faithfulness to standards that are beyond this world, they must have some idea of the world of finance as we live it each day. For modeling to be effective, the children must at least have a rudimentary knowledge of what is being modeled.

2. Parents must practice self-restraint in provision for children. For most of us, the natural inclination is to provide too much. I turn on the news and hear stories of parents who have deprived their children of basic necessities when they could easily have provided for all of their needs, and I simply cannot relate to them.

I don't have trouble with making provision, but I do have trouble saying no. Such difficulty seems to be common with most parents. For the corporate traveler, the problem can be especially pronounced. We often feel guilty because of time spent away from home, perhaps feeling that we do not provide the emotional and spiritual support that we should provide for our family, and we attempt to compensate by making sure all of the material needs are met. Then, we go the second mile to make sure that our children have more than they need.

■ ────────────────────────────────────

If you want to see what children can do, you must stop giving them things. —Norman Douglas

────────────────────────────────────── ■

We may recognize the threat of materialism in our own lives and successfully integrate our value system to the extent that pursuit of financial gain no longer drives us. At the same time, though, often to amend for our real or imaginary shortcomings as parents and spouses, we effectively destroy those desired values in our family by indulging their taste for material goods. But, if our children are to learn a lifestyle of freedom, we cannot continually place the chains of materialism on them.

So often for us, freedom from materialism is a result of a lifelong struggle. It would have been so much easier if, from an earlier age, we had been inculcated with those values which freed us, those values which allowed us to construct a life that is not driven by material consumption. Yet by our provision for our children, we often are condemning them to the same long struggle which we faced. It will be so much better for our children if we practice some self-restraint toward them and help them at an early age to begin to find those same values instead of, by our actions of provision, fueling their innate drive to consume beyond their needs.

3. Parents must teach stewardship to children. What a wonderful gift to provide for children, to allow them to establish values that are much more foresighted than simply measuring a bottom line. By so doing, we allow them to see the big picture, to understand that this world is not the ultimate reality but only a part of the plan that God has for all of us—a plan that encompasses eternity.

Fortunately, many parents have recognized this need. Across America young families are discovering that, along with teaching values of sexual morality, along with teaching children about honesty and integrity, and along with insisting that churchmanship is integrated into life, children need to understand biblical principles of finance. Parents are helping children to understand exactly what dominion means: that God has given us responsibility to live in this world and to enjoy his provision while we are here, and to see that all share in that provision.

We must remember that children are naturally inclined both to accumulate and to share. The lesson of freedom from materialism cannot be learned overnight. This is especially true if it is a new lesson for a child that stands in contrast to all that child has previously been taught.

One of the most popular advertisements in airport gift shops is a poster of a small girl meeting her daddy, suitcase in hand, at the door late at night. The caption beneath reads, "What did you bring me?" Too often, we have enforced that attitude in our children by the way we provide for them. It is very difficult for me, when I travel, not to pick up something to take to my kids every time. That is probably not best for my children, and so I usually choose not to do so. But such is never an easy choice.

The lesson of dependence upon God cannot be learned overnight. Children will not accumulate the knowledge in the same way we do. They are naturally possessive, and they are naturally generous. It is important that parents help children control both of those impulses and place them in the proper perspective of a relationship to God, his creation, and those with whom we share his creation.

Building Bridges

When the story of World War II was reconstructed by historians, it became clear that perhaps the critical decision of the war was when Hitler and his generals pushed too deeply and too quickly into the heart of Russia, overstretching supply lines and outrunning sound military strategy. Any enterprise that moves too far too fast can almost certainly be assured of failure. This is true in the lessons that we try to teach our children as well as it is in military strategy.

In moral issues especially, we often want our children to get the whole picture immediately. We have all seen the father who discovered a new spiritual truth or methodology and immediately rushed home to share the newfound truth with his family. Not only was it important for the father to make the family aware of this spiritual reality, but it was also expected that this new approach to the faith would become normative for the family's behavior. What the children usually learn is: go along with Dad for a while, and then this, too, will pass.

Our children need to see a lifestyle consistently modeled and need to be brought into that way of living one step at a time. If accumulation and consumption have been the child's lifestyle since birth, a hard-and-fast edict from a parent that "We're not going to live that way anymore" is much more likely to engender anger, disbelief, and rebellion than it is to lead the child toward spiritual maturity.

A much better approach, it would seem, consists of building bridges, small spans which move the child gently from where the child is to where you as a parent see the child needs to be. By so doing, our children are given the opportunity to see that our commitment to a lifestyle of responsible stewardship is not a passing fad but rather a lifetime conviction and commitment. At the same time, they are given the opportunity to grow into the reality of the goodness of Jesus Christ in their lives. They are able to learn that they can survive without many of the "necessities" that mark our lives. They also learn to be faithful to our Lord's commands and live in a relationship with him.

Keeping Up with the Jones Kids

What parent has not heard a full inventory of all of the possessions of the neighborhood kids? In the same way that we as adults recognize the pressure to possess and consume at the same level as others in our social strata, so do our children feel a need to match their peers toy for toy, designer shirt for designer shirt, electronic gadget for electronic gadget, and car for car.

Perhaps the pressure for children is even greater than it is for adults. Given the insecurity about position in the world that children so often feel, it is quite natural that possessions become a measuring rod not only of the worth of others, but also of self-worth. The child feels valuable and places himself or herself in the social order according to the amount or type of possessions acquired.

The simple wish to possess is much different from the desire to keep up with friends. The first is based in our natural drive to accumulate and our faith in material possessions, while the second has much more to do with self-image and social insecurity. Each of these questions must be approached in light of the root causes if the problem is to be resolved. Instruction in stewardship and responsibility will have very little effect on the young lady who feels that she can't go to class because she doesn't have the designer clothes that other children in her school are wearing. To be certain, this is a question of stewardship, but one that must be approached by dealing first with the question of adolescent insecurity.

Still, some of the same general guidelines apply. Most important, our children must see what drives our value system. If they see that we are driven by the pressure to keep up with the neighbors, if we have to have a new set of golf clubs every time our playing partner changes his, if our automobile has to be of the same class as the one down the street, if we remark under our breath that someone's suit has become a little bit worn, our children will be quick to note the hypocrisy when we tell them that they should not live by the world's standards. We must consistently model a lifestyle that lets them see that value and our worth as individuals come from the relationships that we form, not from the things that we possess.

And we bring our children along in the same manner. Through years of consistent living and loving, we teach them worth in themselves, we teach them to value other persons for what they are, we help them to learn not to judge by the world's standards.

Beyond the Class Bubble

One of the most important things that we can do for the spiritual well-being of our children is to bring them into contact with people who have not been as financially fortunate as we have. This should be done both through ministry—perhaps letting our children interact with and minister to underprivileged children through a church or social agency on a regular basis—as well as through social contact—encouraging our children to make friends from differing walks of life, and providing them the opportunity to find those friends.

When our children begin to have these contacts, they begin to recognize people as individuals, not as objects measured by financial worth. Helping our children to see people as people will enable them to step beyond the peer pressure for conformity in matters of possessions and allow them to find their own worth in who they are rather than in what they own.

Half a century ago, a German-Jewish theologian wrote a classic study of relationships. Martin Buber's small book, *I and Thou,* argues that the prime source of problems in relationships comes when we begin to treat persons as objects. Objectification occurs when we use people for our own ends, or when we judge people according to their value to us rather than treating them as individuals. When our children count among their acquaintances and friends those who have much less than they do, it is much easier for them to avoid measuring others by material possessions, and they concomitantly stop finding their own worth in what they own. Relationships and treating others as persons rather than objects become the operating paradigm for our children. This context is the beginning of the road to freedom from materialism.

Learning Value

Most young adults are financially ignorant. They do not understand the first thing about money management, budgeting, or living within their means. Studies tell us that financial problems caused by the mismanagement of money are the leading cause of divorce in couples that have been married less than three years. The drive of financial one-upmanship for these young couples who believe they must have it all immediately is a marriage—and life—destroying force.

They do not know anything about money because their parents never took the time when they were children and adolescents to give them instructions in the very basics of personal finance. Parents who would never think of allowing one of their offspring to be married without extensive premarital counseling never bother to talk about the danger of indebtedness. Fathers who are diligent and careful to talk about the privilege and responsibility of sexuality with their children never bother to show those same children how to draw up a family budget. Families that prayerfully provide for the spiritual upbringing of their children never bother to make certain that the children have instructions about stewardship of material things, although that is part and parcel of the biblical message. And then the children, in young adulthood, must pay the cost of that neglect—a cost that is not only financial but also relational, emotional, and often spiritual.

Our children cannot become responsible stewards before God unless they understand some of the basic principles of financial management. In earlier generations, a child understood his or her role in the family by what the child could bring into the family's provision. A young man was called upon either to help with the family farm or business or to find at least summer employment elsewhere. A young woman was also expected to carry her fair load, be it in the house or, often, in the fields.

In today's less agrarian society, our children have less opportunity for earning, but it is up to us as parents to give them the chance to be financial players in their own right. Our children need to participate in the family's finances as well as learn to manage their own budget.

Children need the opportunity to earn. Though employment for younger children outside of the home is by and large neither advisable nor usually possible, younger children should have obligations and opportunities to earn money above and beyond allowance in the home. Such opportunities help them to associate earning with productivity and effort. Earning should be appropriate for the age of the child; younger children should obviously receive less both in terms of responsibility and earning power than older children.

Children need the opportunity to manage. While many children get a chance to earn money, and almost all children get a chance to spend money, very few children learn to manage their money. Parents should begin to help their children at a very early age set up a personal budget. Perhaps a first budget could be divided into very basic categories: tithe, savings, spending, and gifts. The child, from allowance and from earnings, could put certain percentages of their funds into each category on a monthly basis.

As the child grows older, the management categories should be more complex. For children entering their adolescent years, perhaps it would be beneficial for the parents to begin to give the child a certain amount of money each fall to purchase school clothes. For the younger child, even the clothing money would have to be divided up into specific categories (how much for shirts, shoes, etc.), and parental guidance on the shopping trip is a necessity. As the child grows into early adolescence and later teen years, however, the child should have the freedom to budget that money and to make those choices—even choices with which the parent is uncomfortable.

Taking the task of responsibility rarely comes easily for children. Careful management must be learned. Sydney J. Harris stated it well: "We have not passed that subtle line between childhood and adulthood until we move from the passive voice to the active voice—that is, until we have stopped saying, 'It got lost,' and say, 'I lost it.'"

Children need the freedom to fail. The most difficult thing we parents must do is give our children the freedom to learn from their mistakes. We want to insulate and protect them, to keep them from coming into contact with the things that hurt, the bad choices that don't work out. In financial matters, protection of our children from their own foibles, while seemingly the kind thing to do, can have disastrous consequences later on in life.

When the child learns that financial decisions do have an impact, that impulse spending rarely satisfies, and even that going in debt for a much desired object ties up money that at a later date they wish they had, the parent has provided the child with a sound basis for future decision making. We can lecture all we want, we can consistently model a responsible lifestyle, but until the child experiences failure in finance, there is really no way that we can communicate the importance of being a good financial manager.

Permeating all that we do in teaching our children to be good managers of money is the concept of responsible stewardship. Even in the early years, children should learn that their nickel or dime of tithe is given back to God not out of obligation but out of recognition of his provision. It is a confession of our own desire to be good stewards of God's money. As our children reach teenage years, we should help them (while not making final choices for them) to see that the choices we make not only have an impact on the way we live our lives but also raise questions about our responsibility toward God, our church, and our community. Sometimes the lessons don't stick as quickly as we would like, but in later years, the seed that is planted can become a living reality in the lives of our children.

Real Needs

If you have taken the time to pick up this book, the odds are that you are a father who cares very deeply about your family. You are going to provide for them financially. That's really not an issue. The question of indulgence is usually much more relevant than is the question of deprivation, both for us as parents who want to provide and for our children who want to receive. Perhaps in the final analysis we have to ask the question, "What do our children really need from us?" To be certain, they need our physical provision, they need adequate standards of nutrition, comfortable and attractive clothing, a pleasant place to live, and the other material needs that make up their world. Almost all of us provide that.

The temptation to go beyond the needs, to lapse into excess, seems far too often to be a result of a perceived lack in some other area. Just as surely as our children need food and warmth, they also need love and instruction. Just as surely as they need toys for playtime, they need a father who is providing instruction for them. Just as surely as they need clean clothing, they need a father who is an active participant in the whole of their lives. Do not try to buy love. Instead, provide relationship.

Far too often, conspicuous materialism in families is a symptom of a relational sickness, a breakdown in the family unit itself. Many fathers seem to believe that Nintendo and videos are the best baby-sitters that can be found. If the child is occupied with the entire stock of Toys Я Us, the father has no obligation to spend time with the child. Indeed, too many children have seen the relationship break to a point where they would rather spend time with their toys, their games, and their electronic devices than with Dad.

What do your children need most from you? They need your presence. They need you to be an active participant in their lives. When we as fathers take seriously the biblical commands to be full players in the rites of family, then the questions of materialism will probably become much less pressing. Instead, we will discover in the joy of relationship a fulfillment that money simply cannot buy, and our children will discover it too.

WHAT IS IT THAT DAD DOES?

7

You can preach a better sermon with your life
than with your lips.
Oliver Goldsmith

Shortly after I graduated from college, I became good friends with a young woman and her family. One day I asked her what kind of work her father did. She responded that she knew it was something scientific, probably had something to do with the government, but that her father really did not like to talk about it very much. He talked to her about almost every other subject, but never about his work.

Visiting in the home one evening and looking for a topic of conversation, I asked her father about his work. He responded that he was an engineer and told me a little about what he did. Then he invited me to his workplace. Genuinely interested, I responded that I would like to go, and we set a time to visit the plant. A few days later, he met me at the front gate, got my security clearance, and we entered his world.

Immediately, he became a different man, a man obviously in love with what he did. Someone who did not like to talk about his job? Hardly. He introduced me to coworkers, took me through the facility, talked at length about design and manufacturing, and kept me absolutely enthralled for the better part of two hours. It was a fascinating job, and he was a man who was obviously fascinated by it.

Did not like to talk about his work? Somewhere, somehow, an important part of communication had been lost, yet this story does not represent an isolated incident. As we will discuss in a subsequent chapter, today's children often have very little concept of work. Somewhere in the changing roles of a changing society, we as fathers have lost the ability to communicate not only what it is we do, but also why we do it.

From the mists of antiquity right up to the time of the Industrial Revolution, a craft was learned at a father's side. Indeed, by the time of the emergence of the trade guilds in England and throughout western Europe in the late Middle Ages, the means of livelihood became part of a family identity. So we have the beginning of family names linked specifically to a trade or a craft: Miller, Taylor, Smith, Farmer. With the coming of the Industrial Revolution, however, and the emergence of the factory and then the assembly line as the primary places of wage earning, the family began to lose contact with the workplace.

At the same time, the emerging compulsory education standards of the twentieth century meant that mother and father were no longer the primary educators of the children. Instead of the young man learning a craft at his father's workbench and the daughter learning the skills of homemaking beside her mother in the kitchen, the primary task of instructing children

I learned about the strength you can get from a close family life. I learned to keep going, even in bad times. I learned not to despair, even when my world was falling apart. I learned that there are no free lunches. And I learned the value of hard work. —Lee Iacocca

was switched to the school. While we are painting with a broad brush—children throughout the ages have often been separated from their parents for indentured labor, be it slavery or the horrible child labor conditions of the nineteenth century—it must be understood that until the changes of the twentieth century, children understood their parents' roles in the world because the children themselves participated in what the parents did.

We recognize that the general direction of the structural changes in society have set the stage for much good. For example, compulsory education has gone a long way toward reducing illiteracy and ending the horrors of child labor. Likewise, the modern corporation has potential to greatly benefit the family by providing efficient, productive, and high-paying jobs.

However, as Scripture tells us will happen with all human institutions, the structural changes have not lived up to the promise. Many of our schools are as often armed camps as they are institutions of learning. The corporation enslaves as often as it liberates. These changes have been especially hard on the family. The once fully integrated family agenda has been split into bifurcated realms. The child's world is that of the classroom, the school yard, and after-school care. The adult world is that of the factory, the boardroom, and the office. With the exception of the morning or evening meal, those worlds meet only very rarely if at all.

■ ────────────────────────────────

We work to become, not to acquire.
—Elbert Hubbard

──────────────────────────────── ■

What is lost, from the child's perspective, is a glimpse of the bigger picture. The child ends up losing a vision of how everything fits together and has no understanding of how mother or father contribute to the family, much less to the world as a whole. That is a tragic flaw which genuinely threatens the stability of both family and national economy.

Small Eyes See the Workplace

A few years ago, the National Organization For Women initiated a national Take Your Daughters to Work Day. Both mothers and fathers were encouraged to take their daughters into the workplace so that they could catch a glimpse of what it meant to be a productive part of society. Increased familiarity with the workplace, the premise was, would result in young women who were less intimidated by the daunting task of finding a position in the working world.

What a great idea—but one that misses the point. There is a lack of understanding of the workplace not because of institutionalized sexism or stereotyping but because all children—boys and girls—have seen a breakdown in the interconnectedness of the family. Family traditions of all types are no longer passed down from generation to generation. This is especially true of work traditions. We no longer communicate who we are in terms of what we do.

One of the most often mentioned complaints about the youth of today is that they have lost the sense of respect for authority and especially for their parents. Those who level this charge are usually focusing on the outward appearance of respect: the loss of manners in addressing authority, the lack of obedience to parents, and the constant evidence of rebellion.

> *The breakdown of the family is rooted in the loosening of our moral values. Parent-child relationships are built on respect. When we accept unmarried people living together, children out of wedlock, celebrity indiscretions and immorality, we wipe out the foundation of trust and confidence needed by our youth toward the older generation.*
> —Dr. Thomas S. Haggai

Let me suggest that the problem is much deeper than that. Disrespectful actions reflect deeply held attitudes. Many children see no reason to respect their parents today.

At least to some extent, that lack of respect is rooted in a lack of understanding. Children see their father's and their mother's work as absolutely unrelated to their own lives except in terms of the money it provides for them, and many children do not even make that connection.

Whenever possible, our children need to be brought into familiarity with our workplace. This begins long before they take a trip into the office. Conversations about Dad's work should be a regular part of the family discourse. From an early age, the idea that Dad and Mom are doing something important, contributing not only to the family but also to the community and society as a whole, needs to be a part of your child's worldview. As they grow older, they need to be integrated more and more into an understanding of the workplace. In a following chapter, we will deal specifically with the development of a work ethic in our children. Let it suffice to say here that our children need to see our workplace. If company policies preclude regular visits during working hours, they need, at the very least, to be given a conversational knowledge of what it is our jobs demand of us and how our jobs contribute to society as a whole. At that point, our children can begin to respect us not only for who we are in the home, but also for our position in the world at large. They can get a glimpse of the interconnectedness of all we do and who we are. Take our daughters to work? Certainly. But let's take our sons along with them.

Can a Christian Do That?

A friend relates the story of the day his six-year-old found out that the church gave food to needy families. "Why don't they just go to the store and get the food they need?" the child inquired. "Because they don't have any money." "Then why doesn't the store man just give them the food?" "Because he has to make money." "Oh. He must not be a Christian."

Imagine that, a six-year-old with no theology of the marketplace, only an understanding that we as believers are to help others. What followed was a fairly lengthy conversation in which his dad explained that the grocer really was a good man, a Christian who was committed to helping others throughout the community. But for him to stay in business, he could not just open his doors and say, "Anyone who needs food, come and get it." Then the little boy began to get an idea that all answers are not immediately yes or no but sometimes require a bit of development.

We have an obligation to help our children see that Christian faith and means to livelihood are not competing entities. Rather, they are complementary parts of who we are. If our faith has been integrated into the marketplace, then one of the most important lessons that our children can ever learn is that it is very possible for the way we do our jobs to be consistent with the truth of the gospel. If that message is not communicated to our children, then, as they get older and their own jobs become more important to them, their faith will be marginalized and compartmen-

Too often, the civil rights movement is portrayed as a quest for handouts. In its infancy, at least, the movement was about the opportunity to have pride in employment. In one of his addresses on the dignity of work, Martin Luther King stated, "If a man is called to be a streetsweeper, he should sweep streets even as Michelangelo painted, or Beethoven composed music, or Shakespeare wrote poetry.

"He should sweep streets so well that all the host of heaven and earth will pause to say, 'Here lived a great streetsweeper who did his job well.'"

talized. It will not be the overarching, integrating principle that brings all of their lives into a meaningful whole. Instead, it will become a trivial and trite nod to a Christian heritage.

Family Values at the Conference Table

Our children's understanding of the activity of our faith in the marketplace must go beyond a mental comprehension that it is possible to have Christian principles within the free-market system. Children, by and large, are much more interested in the action of our faith than the statement of our beliefs. Declaration of the sovereignty of God in a business means little or nothing to the child when he sees our joy in a competitor's business misfortunes. A prayer for divine blessing upon a transaction or a business day will only confuse the child who sees us driven much more by a philosophy of profit than by an ethic of service.

Our children need to see a value system that informs all we do. When we talk at home about honesty and fair play, then we must also have a consistent ethic of fair play at work. When we teach our children to return good for evil, that their actions are not predicated by the activities of others, we must show a sense of integrity in all that we do in the office.

Children have an uncanny knack for discovering hypocrisy. When they see an inconsistency between the values of the kitchen table and the values of the conference table, it is not to them a simple misdeed. Rather, it is much more complex, and it calls into question the validity of our whole system of belief. They, of course, would never frame it in those words, but that is the issue.

The task before us, then, is to show that there is not a dissonance between who we are as believers and what we do as wage earners. Instead, again, we show that we are a people of faith and that our faith is something that is played out on Monday as well as it is on Sunday, in the boardroom as well as in the home. For us, Christian is not an occasionally descriptive adjective; it is an identity.

A Foundation
for the Family

DR. THOMAS S. HAGGAI
Chairman and CEO,
Independent Grocers Alliance (IGA)

P astor, inspirational speaker, and radio show host were all job descriptions for Dr. Tom Haggai before he came to the helm of the Chicago-based Independent Grocers Alliance. As Chairman and CEO of IGA, an alliance of over 4,000 independent supermarkets, Dr. Haggai must preside over thousands of presidents, each with a personal agenda and outlook. His innovative approach to management has brought a host of changes to the grocery marketplace.

But Dr. Haggai's sense of mission goes far beyond equipping local grocers as effective retailers. He maintains a deep and lasting interest in the health of the families of America. His work at IGA is reflective of that commitment. IGA's motto, "Hometown Proud," is a statement of faith in the values of family and community that are the foundation for America's future.

According to Dr. Haggai, the real hope for families lies within the small business community. He believes that the beginning of the assault on the American family was the Great Society program of the 1960s. "The Great Society was destructive to the male image simply because the family could make as much money without a father present as they could with a father present." In a society where they are no longer needed, "men have lost any sense of their own integrity."

When the man's role in the family collapses, the family itself feels the effect. Intending to build a fail-safe society, what was actually created was a never-safe society. According to Dr. Haggai, what parents have had from the beginning was the responsibility for life, both for creating and sustaining it. The family structure as it had always been understood was destroyed when fathers no longer were responsible for providing. By structuring society in such a way that responsibility was removed from the parents and given to governmental aid programs, the family lost its sense of identity because it lost part of its responsibility for life.

IGA wants to do something about that collapse. All IGA stores are family-owned. When you put a family in business, Dr. Haggai suggests, you allow the family a sense of lovemaking. "We've been so caught up with the sexual/romantic side of love that we forget that problem solving is part of family lovemaking." The chores, the problems, and the tasks of everyday life are where character and values are taught. Within the context of working together, the family finds a sense of unity, a sense of love, and a sense of accomplishment. They become responsible for their own lives.

Dr. Haggai suggests that men today view their businesses much differently from men in the past. Previously, fathers strove to make enough money so that their children would not have to work, so that they would not have to go into the family business. Now they try to make enough so that they can. "There is a new attitude out there about the family participating in work together. We have tapped into that."

Dr. Haggai suggests that the independent grocer is "today's farmer." That is, these family-owned—and family-oriented—businesses are the places where a work ethic, individual drive and determination, and personal creativity allow the owner to prove the margin of success. "We don't insist that you have to do everything our way. What we say is, 'Let us help you do things your way better.'"

Dr. Haggai is also very outspoken about the development of relationships in contemporary society. "Love today cannot withstand the unpleasant. Our society's catch phrase has become, 'I loved him until he did something I didn't like.' Love is acceptance—not changing another for your own satisfaction. True love changes anything it touches for the better."

HEIRS OF THE ROAD WARRIOR

8

It's later than you think.
clock inscription

My friend, Tom, looked across the desk at me. "I have enough Frequent Flyer miles to take my whole family anywhere in the world we want to fly, first class. The problem is, I don't have enough time to take them to the amusement park down the street." Such is the frequent lament of today's businessman. For many men, the world of commerce means a night in a hotel, dinner with clients, and huge balances in the Frequent Flyer account.

It also means that wife and children are back home having the family meal with an empty chair where Dad usually sits. Recent reports on children in the United States seem to focus on their economic situation, with 20 percent of all children now living below the poverty line. For a larger number of children, however, a more serious problem is lack of time with parents. Single-parent families, dual wage earner families, and families in which the father—or the mother—is a frequent traveler have resulted in a situation where children have but a passing acquaintance with one or both of their parents. A recent

University of Maryland study found that in 1993 parents spent 40 percent less time with their children than they did in 1965; seventeen hours a week now compared with thirty hours a week in the sixties.

In the family where both parents work outside of the home, the situation is even worse. Demands of jobs, general household responsibilities, and other obligations effectively rob the parents of time with the children. An August 1994 report showed that working parents spent an average of only eleven minutes of quality time with their children each day—and yet we wonder why children seem to have lost their moral rudder.

Competing Demands

Travel plays a necessary role in the business world. Many jobs require that type of face-to-face encounter that cannot be accomplished through teleconferencing, facsimiles, or E-mail. Some professions require hands-on examination of plants or machinery; *not* to travel is not an option. At the same time, however, business travel has grown and been given priority over other needs in employees' lives, often at the expense of the employees' families.

There is a huge difference in requesting travel from single employees and those with families, but few corporations incorporate that difference into their business plans. The lives of young, single employees are often totally focused upon their careers. Travel doesn't mean separation from family. Instead, it means visiting new places, staying in nice hotels, and eating at good restaurants.

It also means a chance to impress the corporate higher-ups with the employee's work ethic and aggressiveness. It's a chance to climb the corporate ladder, showing activity and experience that can never be garnered while sitting behind the desk. The young employee gains the reputation of the one who never says no when asked to make sacrifices for the company. Over time, travel becomes an ingrained part of the employee's approach to

Closed on Sunday

There it was on Chick-fil-A's ad kiosk in red and white: "Closed on Sunday." Can a restaurant do that? Truett Cathy never intended to make a big deal about closing his restaurants on Sunday, but the subject keeps coming up. "Look at all of the business you're losing," some say. Cathy responds, "I don't believe we've lost any sales in the long run. We usually generate more sales per square foot in six days than most others do in seven."

But why not add the profits of the seventh day? "We feel it is important to give our operators and their employees time to worship if they choose and time with their families." So bypassing that extra day is worth it: "That's how important what we do and what we say are."

business; it becomes *the* method for upward mobility. The habit, then, of three or four nights each week on the road is very difficult to break when a wife and children come onto the scene.

The "road warrior" has become a new business icon. Studies show that even when the frequent traveler comes to resent the stress placed on him by the competing demands of business and family, he very rarely discusses the difficulties he is facing with either his employer or his family. Instead, he stoically marches on, placing both family relationships and job in peril. He finds himself unable to prioritize needs, being constantly torn between his role as provider for the family and his role of participant as husband/father. Out-of-control work habits can make a father absent more often than present even at his own family's dinner table.

At the same time, the wife and children may become "real troopers," refusing to voice their emotional needs because "Dad has to do this for the family." Such refusal may mean a temporary avoidance of conflict. But in reality, it is only postponing an inevitable showdown, a time when choices have to be made between the long-term well-being of the family and the demands of business. It is much better to have the problem stated and examined up front; the earlier the response, the less painful the result will be.

A dangerous lesson is also taught the children in the family. They learn to subjugate relational responsibilities to the demands of employment just as they have observed in their home. And so, the next generation is drawn up into the cycle. What was a habit for the father becomes a tradition for the family.

The View from the Other Side

In a recent broadcast of a network television news magazine, the presentation focused on female officers who were the first women ever assigned to a Navy aircraft carrier. As much as focusing on the officers themselves, the story looked at those who would be left behind—those families who, for an extended period of time, would be without Mom. For the most part, this was an angle of the story I had never before seen.

It was also apparent that few of the husbands and fathers had anticipated that their wives would leave them to take care of the home and the children for an extended period of time. One young man explained, "It's not supposed to be this way: the man is supposed to be the one that leaves. Now I'm supposed to run car pool, keep house, feed the kids, and do my job too. It may be too much to ask." The reporter then asked if that wasn't what women had been doing for ages. The young man then responded with a laugh, "Maybe so, but they're better equipped for it than we are."

That very well may be true, but it doesn't make the task an easy one. When husbands travel, it always makes life more difficult for the wives who are left at home to take care of the house and children. Schedules are pinched, days are longer, and workloads are heavier. From a wife's perspective, there often is an emotional as well as a physical separation.

Of course, the absent husband is missed, and our wives are glad to see us when we return, but that doesn't mean that we can simply walk back in and pick up where we left off. Any time that there is a separation longer than a day or two, there must be a reacquaintance period—a time of getting back in the routine. It becomes especially difficult if travel is so frequent that, by the time husband and wife have gotten acquainted again, it's time to leave once more. Such situations put a great strain on a marriage. There are many ways to ease that strain and to make the transitions less difficult, but we'll get to those in a few pages. It is important to recognize, however, that the strain is there and that transitions always take work.

Dad's travels can be very difficult for the children as well. Just as with wives, the process of reentry can be more difficult than the challenge of separation. Some psychologists suggest that a great part of the tension of reentry comes from the resentment and confusion that a child may have about his relationship to the absent parent. Especially for younger children, it is very difficult to understand why Daddy is leaving. They usually are not capable of making the cognitive connection between their financial well-being and the fact that there is a hole in their lives when Dad is gone. Their confusion is compounded by the fact that the father does become a bit of a stranger during the absence, making it difficult for the relationship to be reestablished.

To be certain, a time of getting reacquainted becomes requisite, but the very first step in crafting a healthy relationship despite travel is recognizing that the travel is probably much less difficult on the traveler than it is on those who are left behind. They have to cover for us. When we finally grasp that, we become much more attentive to the needs of others and less demanding that our own agendas are met.

> ### Concern for the Whole Family:
> ### The Halliburton Company
>
> *It doesn't take long in conversation with Dale Jones to realize that Halliburton is on a different track from most oil field companies. "We have a real concern that our employees are healthy in all areas of their lives." The job is only a part of the employee's life. Halliburton makes a genuine effort to structure work time—an especially precious commodity in the oil field—so that workers can have time with family.*
>
> *More and more corporations are recognizing that, when job demands destroy the home life, the corporation is also the loser, paying the cost in lost time, worker dissatisfaction, and even stress-related medical bills. The far-sighted company is the one that supports the health of the family.*

Setting the Office Agenda

To some extent, we all want to be known as the one at work who will tackle any assignment, who never says no to any job, who is indispensable to the future of the corporation. Most of us want to climb the corporate ladder, but the inescapable fact is that there is very often a tradeoff between corporate success and success within familial relationships. As Christians, all of us know where our priorities must lie. That should be a given rather than an issue.

At the same time, however, we recognize that success in the family and success in the business world are not polar absolutes. That may be how it seems, but in reality they exist on a continuum. At times they can even feed off one another rather than hold each other back. They can build off one another rather than tear one another down. This is the question of balance. It is an important one; in fact, a whole chapter is devoted to it later in this book. In these pages, however, let's draw the issue a bit more tightly and focus on the trade-off between travel and family time.

There are really two issues involved in determining travel amount: one is personal, one corporate. On a personal level, we must ask the question of how much travel is necessary and

---

In his biography of Nelson H. Rockefeller, J. E. Persico relates an experience of Rockefeller's priorities. During a Saturday staff meeting in the Governor's home, they reviewed the drafts of a budget proposal that was to be delivered to the state legislature.

As budget director Norman Hurd was explaining a passage, Rockefeller's son, Mark, came into the room. They all soon heard the Governor respond, "Yes, that's right, Marky. That's a two. And that number is a nine. See, we're on page twenty-nine."

Persico continues, "Nelson Rockefeller was passing along an unspoken lesson learned from his own father." Perhaps we do not have the position or authority to take our children into the boardroom, but we do have the divine right to take time for them.

An even better story is told of Theodore Roosevelt and his family's reign in the White House. During an important meeting, Roosevelt's daughter, Alice, broke into the conference room and began playing. A staffer complained about the intrusion, and Roosevelt responded, "I can be President of the United States or I can control Alice. I cannot possibly do both."

---

how much travel we do simply because that is the way we prefer to do the job. I find travel to be a very effective way to do my job. In addition to the face-to-face relationship building that is so much a part of what I do, travel time can also be productive time for catching up on desk work. If I have no appointments before 11:00 A.M., I can focus on difficult projects without worrying about interruption from the telephone or people dropping by my office. After the last appointment of the evening, I can turn on a baseball game, pull the paperwork back out, and get more done in one night than I would in three or four mornings sitting behind my desk. Without the responsibilities of home, I usually come back from my time on the road with a great sense of accomplishment, a feeling of relaxation, and a measure of vigor with which to tackle the tough problems that will meet me at the office the next morning.

The question for me, then, is am I willing just to leave the family responsibilities to my wife? I must honestly ask myself if the trip is necessary. To be certain, there are occasions when travel is a necessity, but there are other times when perhaps the job can be done just as effectively from behind the desk—and the man who travels on business must be constantly aware of striking a balance. Striking that balance may, at times, mean having a frank discussion with an employer.

There are certain times when an "I will not travel" is altogether appropriate. Birthdays of children, baptisms, and first days of school can hold a higher priority in your life than other days. If at all possible, we should be home on those days. That may mean cutting a trip somewhat short; it may mean a red-eye flight across country; or it may mean rescheduling a nonessential meeting. Your children will see and recognize and appreciate your commitment, and they will gain a better understanding of the importance of relationships and the priorities in your life.

Very few individuals seem actually good at turning down assignments at work; it is natural to want to look the very best and to be the most aggressive person in the shop. More and more, however, employers are recognizing that domestic peace and strong family relationships benefit the company. Employees with lower levels of stress on the home front often show greater productivity in the office. It's worth the company's while to recognize the necessity of time at home with family.

On a corporate level, if you are in a decision-making position, you do your company a great service when you draft policies that strengthen family relationships. The company that exacts every last ounce of energy from its employees by demanding that they are constantly on the road will almost certainly pay the price in decreased productivity, worker burnout, and employee turnover. The wise manager is the one who recognizes the reality and the importance of the family in the life of the worker.

For many men, however, the road has to remain a constant companion. Certain types of jobs just cannot be done any other way. Concrete steps that we can take, while still not a substitute for Dad's presence, nonetheless make positive provisions during the time of separation. Especially with children, for example, preparation for the time away is extremely important. To find out around the breakfast table that Dad is getting ready to be gone for a week denigrates the importance of the child's role in the family and suggests a lack of fatherly affection for the child.

How you prepare your children for your absence depends largely upon their age. An older teenager needs to know not only your destination and length of stay, but also the purpose of the trip. It is important that they understand why you are doing what you are doing. When they gain a recognition of the necessity of the trip, it will help them manage their feelings about your absence, as well as prepare them to make the same type of sound judgments about time and family when they are older.

At the same time, the discussion of the separation should probably cover responsibilities that the teenager is to assume while you are away. Whether that means completing some of the tasks that usually fall onto your job list or relieving Mom from some of her responsibilities so that she is free to help out in other areas, older teenage children can, in a very real sense, participate in the livelihood of the family by enabling you to do your job more effectively. The sense of responsibility thereby gained is of great benefit to both the family and the teenager.

A younger child should also be made aware of your impending time away and its implications for the family. A discussion of destination and length of trip, complete with the breaking out of atlases and maps, gives the child a sense of participating with Dad in both job and travel. For toddlers, with a less developed sense of time, a father's travel can be tied to specific events in the child's life: "When you get up in the morning, Daddy will be on the way to the airport. Tomorrow night when you and Mom go out for pizza, Dad will be meeting with business friends in San Diego. Right before you go to John's soccer game on Saturday, Daddy will be back home to go with you." Such an approach provides a younger child the chance to identify with a father's absence.

For our wives also, preparation for separation is imperative. Although last-minute trips do come up, whenever possible, trips should be calendared as far in advance as is feasible. Do not make her squeeze trip information out of you. Well beforehand, prepare detailed itineraries including flight plans, hotels, and phone numbers.

Because your time away does cause a change in the family plans and approach to activities, be a willing partner in planning coverage; don't just drop it in her lap with an "I will be gone next week. Here is the number where I will be staying." Instead, help her design the family plans for the time when you will have to be away. Make arrangements for the children's pick-up from school, for example. Your participation in the preparation for your time apart will strengthen the bond and make the time of separation easier.

Out of Sight, but Not Out of Mind

I was sitting in a boardroom in Memphis. I looked at the two legal pads of the man sitting next to me. One was covered with neat handwriting in red ink. "Dear David," it began. I looked at Chuck Staley, Director of Real Estate at Anderson University, with a questioning expression.

At our first break, Chuck explained. "I hate being away from my family, but I know that sometimes it can't be avoided. I decided some time ago that I would write my son a letter on each trip just to let him know I was thinking of him." Somehow, I do not think David will ever question his father's commitment to him.

During the time apart, it is imperative that close contact be maintained. Daily telephone calls are, of course, requisite, but any extended separation (that is, anything longer than about three days) requires at least a short postcard. It is quite easy just to pick up the phone—sometimes that's just the way to overcome the boredom of a hotel room. It is quite another thing to go to the trouble of articulating your thoughts on paper. Your wife and children, however, will recognize and appreciate the extra mile that you have gone. And again, children will see that relationships sometimes take a little work. What better gift from your travels could they be given?

Getting Reacquainted

Trip's over; we're home. We walk through the door and pick up right where we left off. Well, not really. Report cards came home three days ago, and one child is seeming to have a little trouble with math. The oldest daughter has traded boyfriends (again). But you have only been gone a week.

Nonetheless, a lot of water has gone under the bridge since you left. To assume that we will walk back into a changed family situation and pick up where we left off really borders a little bit on egocentrism, thinking the family revolves around Dad. Too often we do not realize that there needs to be a time of readjustment. Smaller children, especially, need to get used to having Dad around again. With older children, issues that may have come up while you were gone and been settled by the present parent do not particularly need to be rehashed, but you would like to know how *that* decision was made. Your wife has been wrestling car pool and chasing runaway dogs all week, and the first thing you want to do is walk in and tell her about the great view from your hotel room?

No, coming home does require a period of getting acquainted again. The way that you handle this transition will go a long way toward setting the family agenda for the time that you are home. It will also make your next period of separation easier to approach.

The first trap we must avoid is the "buy my way back into good graces." So many fathers, with guilt fed by long periods away, want to walk through the door with a bundle of gifts for every person in the family. While that is, on occasion, certainly justified, it should never become standard procedure. Once the children begin to associate your return with an automatic gift, the gift rather than the person can very quickly become the focus.

As much as possible, the first minutes home after the hellos should be spent catching up on news, hearing the stories and adventures from the children, the wife, and the father, and focusing on pleasantness. It is *not* the time to settle the unresolved issues of the week. To walk back into the middle of family difficulties does absolutely nothing to reestablish relationships. The entire family should understand the ground rules: the first hours that anyone returns from a trip are to be hours of enjoying each other's company. Major issues which need attention can wait until after the first meal or until the next morning. Such an approach requires both diligence and discipline, but it certainly makes life more pleasant for everyone.

Perhaps there is one area where a gift is regularly appropriate: to your wife. After all, she is the one who carries the load while you are gone. This does not have to be some present purchased while you are away. It can be as simple as "If you'd like to get out of the house a while, I'll take care of the kids" or taking the family out for dinner. While a restaurant meal might be the last thing you desire after a week in hotels, this may be the first opportunity that your wife and children have had to get away and relax since you have been gone. The home-cooked meal can wait until tomorrow—and then maybe you need to help prepare it.

Support for the Home Troops

There are a thousand variations and takes on the old adage "Behind every good man there stands a woman." Cliché, trite, but so often true. Nowhere is the concept more valid than it is in the family where the father must often be on the road. Actually, it is more than just a good woman. If the family of a traveling father is to be successful, it takes a family-wide effort; everyone has a role to play; everyone has responsibilities for seeing that the relationships are maintained in a strong fashion and that the basic business of family is done.

Too often we as men place the priority upon our work. It is not just that we give more of our time to our work; it is also that we give attention to all of the details that make our businesses run smoothly. The successful businessman makes sure his office is automated with state-of-the-art equipment, that there is adequate staffing to meet the demands of the work, and that the company fully supports the employees as they try to complete their assignments.

Conversely, we often tend to think that the home front will run just fine on autopilot, that we can make do with second best, and that the relational tasks of the family will get done with a minimum of attention. When we relegate our family to second-class status, we are as likely to be unsuccessful in the business of family as any company would be at its business if given inferior equipment and insufficient staffing.

The wise husband does everything in his power to facilitate the success of his family. That may mean purchasing appliances that make meal preparation easier when you are not around to help out with the other family chores. It may mean hiring some extra household help. It may mean a lot of little things, but what it most certainly does mean is that you work hard at relationships, that in the time when you are not on the road you do not bury your head in the television, hide in the study with take-home work, or disappear to the golf course every time the family turns around. All of those activities may be restful for you and may help you maintain your pace in a fast-moving world, but they mean that you have taken even more time away from your family.

If we are genuinely to be full players in the rites of family, it means that we must make choices and set priorities. It also means that we must choose to spend the time necessary to build the strong and solid foundation for our family that will not be washed away by the rains of separation.

THE FOUNDATION FOR THE FUTURE: DISCIPLINE IN THE HOME

9

I praise loudly, I blame softly.
Catherine the Great, Empress of Russia

During graduate school, I refereed football to pay the bills. One season during our official's chapter meeting, the chapter president instructed us that we were instituting a new policy on fighting during ball games. If a fight broke out between two or more players, we were to blow our whistle, throw a flag, tell the players to quit fighting—and then stand back until it ended. It seems that, the week before, a local referee had stepped in to stop a fight between two players, separated them, ejected them from the game, and escorted each one to the sideline. By Monday morning, a lawsuit had been filed against the official by the parents of one of the boys, suggesting that he had deprived the young man of his right to participate in the game.

Wait a minute. Something is wrong with this picture. No wonder we are having trouble with discipline in our schools.

The whole purpose of athletics grows out of an understanding of the value of competition. Student athletes are to learn the game and the nature of teamwork, but all of these lessons occur within the context of discipline, of learning to direct those competitive fires toward a desired end. Yet here were parents who, by filing a suit, were basically arguing that high school athletics should be disciplineless competition.

Disciplineless competition. Perhaps a picture of corporate America today? Disciplineless competition is precisely what happens when we lose sight of the big picture, when competition becomes an end unto itself, when we seek to win at all costs. The basic premise of the free-market system has never been to win at any cost. Rather, it has been that disciplined competition assures that higher quality goods will be available to a greater number of people. When we see the big picture, we understand our role and our part in the delivery of goods and services.

Even very young children need to be informed about dying. Explain the concept of death very carefully to your child. This will make threatening him with it much more effective. —P. J. O'Rourke

---

For the question of discipline in the home, however, most parents—and consequently, most children—don't ever get the big picture. Discipline is seen not as a long-term objective but as an immediate end to itself—"Correct the problem right now; we'll worry about the big picture later." Consequently, correction and punishment are arbitrary and inconsistent, and instruction is absent. Children never grow to understand the objective of discipline and, therefore, resent it. Parents have little or no philosophy of discipline simply because they don't understand where the whole process is going.

The problem becomes especially pronounced when the father—the traditional figure of discipline—spends little time at home because of job and travel obligations. For many of my generation, the words "Just wait 'til your father gets home" were a threat never lightly taken. The time of Dad's homecoming was often not an eagerly anticipated exercise of welcome but rather something dreaded because punishment awaited when he learned of the mischief of the day. There was no doubt about it; Dad was in charge of punishment.

In this day of long hours at the office, Frequent Flyer accounts, and often absent fathers, the roles in the family easily become confused. It is, therefore, imperative that we think through the nature of discipline, that we do have an idea of the big picture. If we want our children to grow up to be effective members of the Christian community, then we need to have some idea of where we are going. As in business, "those who have no destination in mind will likely get there."

A Biblical Perspective on Discipline

The question of the role and nature of discipline is by no means a new one. No issue is discussed in wider or more varied settings in Scripture than is the issue of the instruction and correction of children. Interestingly enough, however, with the exception of a few notable examples like the childhood of Moses and a brief interlude in the life of Jesus, we are given very few examples of what it means to bring up a child in the ways of God. Most of what we receive are instructions to do so; the details are, by and large, left open.

What we do get from Scripture is a broad foundation for an understanding of the role of discipline in the home. The admonition, "Train up a child in the way he should go, and when he is old he will not depart from it" gives us a clear indication that this is an outcome-based discipline. That is, discipline in the home is always directed toward a desired goal.

Making such a claim for a result orientation, however, requires some qualifiers.

By outcome-directed discipline, we do not mean that we focus on our objective to such an extent that the process becomes important only in terms of what it can deliver. What it does mean is that we see the big picture, that we do not discipline for the sake of discipline, that we do not correct our children only to show who is boss—although that, at times, is a part of it. Instead, we are looking at the full scope of what it means to be a child of God, and we are structuring our children's lives in such a way that this objective is always before us. It all fits into a pattern of being a meaningful whole.

From a scriptural perspective, the objective is clear: Children need to obtain spiritual as well as relational maturity. The interaction between parent and child, then, in that time of discipline becomes more than just bonding and affection. Instead, it is directed toward the end of maturity and wisdom. Children are to learn obedience, for that will quell a stubborn and self-willed spirit. Children are to learn the Word of God in order to avoid sinfulness (Ps. 119:9–11). Children are disciplined and corrected because discipline produces a harvest of life and peace (Heb. 12). Each aspect of discipline has a goal.

> *By discipline men are placed in subjection to the laws of mankind, and brought to feel their constraint. This, however, must be accomplished early. For example, children are first sent to school not so much with the object of their learning something, but rather that they may become used to sitting still and doing exactly as they are told. And this to the end that in later life they should not wish to put actually and instantly into practice anything that strikes them.* —Immanuel Kant

---

And those goals extend beyond the immediate needs of child and family. It is important to note that in the even broader picture, the process of bringing up children is not only about the child's well-being, but about the well-being of society as a whole. The covenant promise of God to the children of Israel in Exodus 20, "Honor your father and your mother, that your days may be long upon the land which the Lord your God is giving you," is not a promise to an individual. We have all known very obedient, wonderful Christian children whose lives were cut short by illness or accident. They do not all live to old age. This passage is not directed to that issue. Rather, it is a corporate promise, a statement to the people of Israel that if the children of the community are faithful and obedient to the parents (and the responsibility to see that they are falls on the parents!), then the community can anticipate prosperity.

The specifics of discipline are not outlined for us in the Bible. Scripture instructs that we are to have a disciplined household, but the "how" of that directive is left to be determined within our individual circumstance. That silence undoubtedly occurs for good reason. We live in a different age. It would make very little sense to try to impose the discipline of a twentieth-century B.C. Bedouin tribesman's family on the home of a twentieth-century A.D. urban corporate executive. The needs, expectations, and realities simply are not the same. The freedom that God gives us to craft our own methods and approaches within the context of Christian freedom is a hallmark of New Testament faith.

Discipline in the Executive's Household

While the ultimate objective may remain the same, the needs and methods of different ages and cultures call for different approaches to the question of family discipline. Even within the context of twentieth-century America, the life situations of individual families and the relationships within those families mean that there may be many answers to the same question.

The cardiac surgeon with four children in Minneapolis will have a home life structured differently than a rural, south Texas automobile dealer with one child. Neither approach may be wrong or right—or even better—but each approach may be effective for the particular life situation in which the family finds itself.

> *There's nothing wrong with teenagers that reasoning with them won't aggravate.* —Anonymous

We should always be open to the working of God where we are in every circumstance. As said before, perhaps the most important lesson to learn from Scripture is that God is bigger than our circumstance, and that he can take us wherever we are and make us productive members of his kingdom—if we are only willing to listen and to follow.

Certain problems and concerns, however, do seem to be shared by a large number of businessmen today. More often than not, these questions seem to center around the issue of roles in the family: Who makes the discipline decisions? Who enforces the discipline decisions? Who sets the overall discipline agenda for the family?

Many of us grew up under the shadow of a "Dad's in charge of discipline" mentality. The father made the rules, and the father enforced the rules. The mother's job was to simply keep record of violations when the father was not present. As head of the household, it was thought that Dad was the only one who could make the calls.

What does such a division of duties suggest about relationships? It almost certainly indicates to children that Mom and Dad are not equal partners in the marriage. It may also prevent each parent from having a fully integrated relationship with the children. For example, if Dad is always the enforcer, does that not automatically push Mom into the nurturing/comforter role and deny that to the man?

Does this separation of duties perspective fit the biblical model? I really do not think so. The few images that we do have of the raising up of children in Scripture show women playing a vital role in the discipline of the children. Note especially the mother and sister of Moses and the women in Timothy's life. When we approach discipline as strictly a father's prerogative, it denigrates the role of the mother in the household. A "Wait 'til your father gets home" mentality basically says that the mother is not capable of being a full partner in the discipline of children, a perspective that is simply not biblical.

Even on just a practical level, such an approach can be very difficult for the family. When the father is seen as a returning agent of correction, children will soon learn to dread his return from the office or an out-of-town trip rather than eagerly anticipate time with him. When Dad is required to walk through the door and straighten out the problems, very little time ends up being devoted to the building up of relationships.

There are times, of course, when the mother and father need a time of discussion and reflection before correction is given to a child. This, however, is less a "Wait 'til your father gets home" than it is a "We need to think about this one for a while."

At the same time, however, the executive father cannot absent himself from his children's discipline. In our day and time, it is probably more common that the mother is more involved in the upbringing of the children and, consequently, becomes the agent of discipline. Then, Dad comes home and gets to enjoy the good times because Mom has taken care of all of the problems already. Dad becomes the hero who rescues the children from the clutches of the evil mother. Quite honestly, that is a role that's fun to play sometimes, but the children's relationship with their mother always pays a price.

In well-balanced family relationships, Dad must be neither the enforcer nor the hero. Rather, he must be a full partner with the mother in assuring that the children grow up to be the kind of young men and young women who will bring honor to themselves, their family, and the kingdom of God.

A Broader Perspective: Value-Based Discipline

A few years ago a friend of mine relayed his understanding of the way to raise children: "You have to let them see the goal, to know where you're going. You don't make children *mind.* You make them *cooperate.*" No. I'm sorry, but that is not the way it works. A three-year-old does not see the big picture. I am more concerned that he mind than that he cooperate. Nor will I always explain the "why" to a ten- or eleven-year-old, or even to a teenager. There are times for explanations; at other times, children just need to do what they are told.

At the same time, however, I think there was a kernel of truth in my friend's far-flung idealism. Discipline and the rearing of children are not random adventures. Instead, they involve a process that is going somewhere. As parents, at least, we need to see how the paving stones all fit together to make a pathway, and we need to have some understanding of where that pathway is going. There are, to be sure, plenty of unexpected twists, turns, rises, and dips along the way, but we are nonetheless progressing toward an ultimate goal—and each step we take should be carrying us toward that destination.

As much as possible, the children should be allowed to participate in both articulating the final objective and determining the path to get there. Whenever we go on a family vacation, the entire family joins in on the planning of the trip. We pull out tour guides, maps, and almanacs, decide where we are going to go, and together we chart the path.

The journey of family should be the same kind of joint effort. As much as possible, the family needs to understand not just what we are doing, but why we are doing it. This not only cues them in on what we are about as family, but it also prepares the children for the day when they will be making such decisions on their own, the time when they will be charting the path for their own family. It gives them the equipment to make that type of decision. It is a wise parent who calls on the children to be participants in the process of child rearing. Sometimes that may even mean letting children make their own determination about appropriate punishment for misdeeds and appropriate rewards for exceptional behavior. But, when the whole family is involved, each move leads toward emotional and spiritual maturity.

The most effective corporations are those that come into business with a teamwork approach. Employees are made to feel a part of the effort not only in accomplishing the agenda but in setting the agenda and determining the route to achievement. When employees "buy into ownership" in such a way, the corporate product becomes their product. This is no less true in the family. The child who has bought into the process will feel a sense of ownership in seeing that the family accomplishes the task that God has set before them.

More Is Caught Than Taught

It is very important to make children feel that they are helping to build the path to success for the family. At the same time, however, it is of critical importance that the children feel that you are willing to walk the path with them. There are so many areas where the rules seem to apply to everyone but Dad. How many fathers talk about the importance of spiritual nurture for their children yet seek to accomplish that nurture by dropping the kids off at church on Sunday, never deeming it necessary for they themselves to participate? How often are children lectured about honesty and yet see Dad conduct shaky business deals? Do we have the right to talk to our kids about self control if we constantly lose our temper with our wife and children? More than they need most of the things on their list of necessities, children need to see a father who consistently models the same principles that he insists are the guidelines for the family.

Education, as often observed, is an expensive thing. It is so; but the paying for lessons is the smallest part of the cost. If you would go to the price of having your son a worthy man, you must be so yourself. —Anna Letitia Barbauld
"On Education," Miscellaneous Pieces in Prose (1773)

Our children need to see a lifestyle of discipline from us. When we chafe at authority or disparage a boss behind his back, we teach our children that being a mature adult means refusing to submit—at least in spirit—to authority.

My dad used to relate a story from my early childhood: one day he instructed me to sit down, and I refused. After a second refusal, he explained to me that I would sit down immediately. Probably fearing for my physical well-being, I obeyed, but as I sat down I responded, "I may be sitting down on the outside, but I'm still standing up on the inside." If children see a rebellious nature and stubborn spirit portrayed in the lives of parents, then the parents have lost the whole battle of helping them to become mature Christians. Genuinely accepting discipline means we recognize authority and its vital role in life, not just that we obey in order to save our skin.

Management by objectives works if you know the objectives. Ninety percent of the time, you don't.
—Peter Drucker

If we are to model discipline for our children, they must also see self-discipline from us. While we cannot be held to a standard of perfection, and while our children should not be allowed to point out flaws in our behavior every time we correct theirs, we nonetheless have an obligation to live the type of disciplined lives that we are trying to impose on our children. The old "Do as I say, not as I do" simply does not work. Children quickly see inconsistency and hypocrisy.

Conversely, when our children see modeled the same type of discipline in our lives that we expect from them, their attitude about their behavior is usually much more constructive. If good actions, a positive outlook, wholesome relationships, and self-discipline are just a part of everyday life, then it will be much easier to inculcate those same values in our children. When those things become the norm rather than the extraordinary, our children are much more likely to assimilate those values, and their lives will be different in the long run. So many times we meet adults who struggle to master some element of self-discipline while offering the explanation, "That just wasn't part of my life when I was growing up." Enforced discipline in childhood usually means self-discipline in adulthood.

We make the formulation of values and discipline so much easier for our children when we establish an atmosphere in which the positive Christian attributes are just a part of the way we do family. In our home we make it a regular practice to read the last verses of the fifth chapter of Galatians. We can then evaluate how we are doing as individuals by measuring ourselves against Paul's listing of the fruit of the Spirit. Knowing that there is a standard to which we are held helps children understand that the lifestyle we are pursuing is not arbitrary but is part of our identity as a Christian family.

Celebration of the Moment

Children need structure. They need to understand that home is a place of safety and values, a place where everyone accepts you for who you are and looks forward to seeing what you are going to become. They need to be assured of the stability of the family unit and of the constancy of its values.

At the same time, children need spontaneity, the surprising change of pace that brightens their day and keeps everything from becoming monotonous. Very often, however, discipline, structure, and stability stand in conflict with freedom and spontaneity. It is very important that we structure spontaneity into our lives. That does not mean, of course, that we schedule a time each day when we will be spontaneous. That much structure kills the spirit of freedom.

What we must do, however, is be ready to celebrate the joy of the moment, the wonder of the unexpected. Our children must have a firm understanding that discipline and fun are not antonyms; there really doesn't have to be a lesson or a point to everything that we do together as family. Sometimes we can do something just because it is enjoyable. Whether it is renting a movie of juvenile humor and laughing our way through it with our kids or stopping beside the road just because we've spotted a creek that looks like it would offer a good swim, a sense of living in the moment communicates to our children that the joy of living is part of our identity as children of God.

Celebration of the moment also means that we take those time-out moments with our children when they ask for them, not just when they have been structured into our day. Stopping to look at a sunset, the one quick kick of a soccer ball as we walk out the door on the way to work, the smile and the word for a boy and his dog all add up to a profound, if not articulated, statement that "You and your life are important to me." Our children must always understand that when it comes to seeing the big picture, we have never really lost track of who they are.

A Covenant of Discipline

Our youngest child and I have a special agreement. When she asks, "May we go sit on the roof and talk?" I will drop whatever I am doing at any time to fulfill that request. She also understands that her part of the obligation is that she never asks at a time when it's obviously going to be inconvenient for me unless it is of critical importance. It's all right to go to the roof just for a visit, but that request needs to come when I have time to do it.

To this point at least, neither of us has ever had to back down on our agreement. That is our special place and our special time. It is a covenant that we have toward each other, a covenant to be open and honest with our feelings, to help each other work through the problems that are a part of a child's— and an adult's—life. It is one place she knows she can always count on me.

We have other special covenants in our home. Covenants of discipline can be an effective part of any Christian's household. A covenant of discipline is an agreement by the family members, both adults and children, that assesses the long-term goals of the children in the family. Within that covenant, there may be some very general ideas such as what type of person the child wants to be when he or she grows up. The covenant should include the qualities of maturity that are the objective of every Christian—to be a person of integrity, to be a person of good reputation, to be a person who cares about God and other people. But it can also include some fairly specific life goals. Some family covenants may include a career objective: one child may want to be a veterinarian, one child a heart surgeon, another a builder. All those are appropriate to be included in the family's covenant of discipline.

The second part of the covenant of discipline is a recitation of what each family member will do to help fulfill the commitment to those goals. From a parent's perspective, it might be a promise that not only will we see that their physical needs are met, but also that the child will be required to deal honestly with all family members, that the child will have to be responsible for certain tasks. It might include promises about activities that will help the child move toward career goals. "If you really want to be a veterinarian, we'll let you have a pet or show animals which will help you decide if that is really your life's calling."

From a child's perspective, the covenant of discipline requires promises to try to live up to the family standards and to do their part in school, in leisure activities, and in other parts of their life in order to achieve the objectives that are stretched before them. For developing Christian character, it might be a promise that during fifth grade the child will keep a spiritual diary chronicling his or her spiritual journey.

To be sure, objectives change, goals change, methodologies change. But the covenant is open and constant. The promise that whatever the task before them, all family members will participate: Mom, Dad, brother, sister—everyone—to make sure that the family is a unit and family members as individuals achieve the goal of "the high calling of God."

Family Values
for the Whole Family

DR. JOEL MORRISETT
Scientific Director,
NMR Spectroscopy Laboratory
Professor of Medicine and Biochemistry,
Baylor College of Medicine

As we discuss values and the development of values in our children, we often see the process as something that is passed on from one generation to the next. For Dr. Joel Morrisett and his family, Christian values are less something that is passed on than that which grows and develops within the context of the family. For almost a quarter of a century, Dr. Morrisett and his family have been members at Rice Temple Baptist Church in Houston, Texas. Dr. Morrisett is Professor of Medicine and Biochemistry at Baylor College of Medicine as well as Scientific Director of the NMR Spectroscopy Laboratory there. He and his wife, Mary, have seven children ranging in age from nine to twenty-four. How do parents of a family of that size instill values in their children?

"At least in the beginning, it probably was not as carefully planned as you might think," states Joel. At one point during the early years of their marriage, the Morrisetts hosted a Christian couple, Jim and Wilma High, who were in Houston for a Lay Witness Mission, a weekend series of small-group encounters and revival services. The Highs asked the Morrisetts if they had any type of regular family time. With the response that they did not, they were encouraged to begin one. "When we started having a family time before the children went to bed each night, it served as a real unifying point for the entire family." It is within the context of those family times, especially in the early formative years of two through twelve, that the values of the family are developed and articulated.

One of the biggest challenges was developing a family time that was meaningful for all ages of children, from the oldest to the youngest. But from the outset, it was important for the Morrisetts that the issues of family be approached together. All of the children together were given the opportunity to share their problems, their concerns, and their triumphs so that individual life challenges could be prayed about corporately, so that a real feeling of family was nurtured.

"The older ones serve as models and examples for the younger ones, and therein lies an important key. Often it is the oldest child with whom you have the most problems, partly because the first child tends to be very strong willed and partly because parents are making their first major parenting decisions with that child and have to take some hard stands on issues." Within that context then, younger family members begin to see the pattern emerging when they discover that Mom and Dad are not going to back down from what they believe is right. With each succeeding child, the standards have been part of the family for a longer period, and there is less challenge of those standards. "The family time for us has been a central mechanism for instilling Christian values.

"A second important time for building self-esteem and personal worth in children is the time we spend together during the evening meal. We've always tried to make that time a priority. It takes extra time and energy to convene our complete family for the meal, but Mary and I feel that this effort pays rich dividends, not only in equipping our children with tools to handle life well, but to build a storehouse of family memories that can be recalled in later years as they begin to raise their own families and train their children. We use this meal time not only for conversation about the difficulties of life, but also as just time to talk, share, and become a part of each other's lives." Joel points out that it is particularly helpful for the younger children to get "the wide slice of life" as they hear older brothers and sisters discuss their days at school and other activities.

One of the real challenges that any Christian family faces is the threat that the instilled values will be destroyed once the child leaves home. We've all heard stories of the young man or young woman who has been raised in a protective environment with the very best of Christian values, only to be so overcome by the world beyond the home that those values went straight out the window. Along the same line, we could recall the child raised in a strict environment who finally escapes to college and, perhaps for no other reason than to prove independence, does everything possible to repudiate the morality of youth.

Given the size of the Morrisett family and the strong moral upbringing that the children received, you might expect at least one of these children to reject instilled family values and to chart his or her own path into the world. At this point, that hasn't happened. What is it that this family does to make sure that these values take and are fully integrated into their children's lives?

"It is absolutely essential that the values of the home become the values of the children," Joel relates, "and I think that how we use our time together largely determines whether or not that will happen." The Morrisetts recognize the danger of reaction or rebellion after a child is "out from under the bubble" and no longer under their direct control. It is quite possible that if you spoon-feed religion to your children and do not encourage and stimulate honest questions about life's choices, they will accept parents' answers at home, but may discard them when they get out on their own. Again, for the Morrisetts, the answer comes in the structure of their family time together. By bringing the whole family into the discussion, for any issue, be it dating, premarital sex, or substance abuse, several perspectives are represented within the family, and what the parents teach is put to a rather rigorous test. When younger children see biblical principles applied by their parents and validated in their older siblings, these children find it relatively easy to follow these principles.

"I think it's that balance that is important." Joel and Mary do not do all the speaking in the family sessions. All of the children are encouraged to voice their opinions, give their views, and share how the principle under discussion might apply to them. In that way, each child has a part in developing and assimilating basic Christian values.

These values are never drawn in abstract. The approach is never "It's wrong to do this. End of discussion." Instead, the family works diligently to make sure every family member understands why a particular position is taken, whether it concerns alcoholic beverages, tobacco, television, interpersonal relationships, money, or marriage. By approaching issues in this way, each child gains a sense of ownership in the standards of the family.

Family involvement in the development of standards, however, does not mean that the majority rules when it comes to following those standards. For the Morrisetts, it is not just a matter of Mom or Dad saying it or of all the children agreeing with it. Instead, the final question is always, "What does God's Word have to say about it?" By seeking answers to questions within the context of Scripture, the Morrisetts find a firm foundation upon which to build family standards.

"We use God's Word as a basis, and then we let our children ask the hard questions." When the family begins to develop its understanding of right and wrong as a corporate body, a sense of responsibility for one another is then engendered, and that perhaps is the greatest benefit of all. To be sure, sibling rivalry still exists, but so do care and concern for the spiritual well-being of the other family members. At that point, values have become not what you do, but who you are.

CHURCHMANSHIP **10**

What this country needs is a man who knows
God other than by hearsay.
Thomas Carlyle

This is a chapter that my pastor made me
write. Well, not exactly *made* me. Perhaps "strongly suggested"
is a better term. As we began visiting about the scope of this
study, he did ask, "What are you going to say about churchmanship?" After we had talked for a few minutes longer, I
realized it was impossible to really address the role of Christian
men in contemporary society without dealing with the question
of how we as men relate to the church as a whole.

As this chapter began to come together, the question kept
forcing itself on me: Where have all of the great churchmen
gone? Where are all of those men who have a genuine and
burning passion for the church as the body of Christ? When I
was a young boy, the men who were my role models—those
whom I trusted for guidance and wisdom—were my Sunday
school teachers or the leaders of our boy's mission organization.
Are there still men like that out there today?

They are still there. They still open God's Word each Sunday
morning with the boys and girls and men and women of
America. They are men like Truett Cathy, Founder and CEO
of Chick-fil-A, who has taught a boys' Sunday school class for
the last thirty-eight years. Men like Cliff Johnson who for

many years made sure that every third and fourth grader in the Sunday school of Calvary Baptist Church in Waco, Texas, understood that Christ loved them and died for them. They are men like attorneys Cass Fritz and Thom Sanders who are helping their communities stretch the definition of the traditional church by finding new and innovative ways to minister to those who simply have never before been open to the gospel message. They are out there, all right, and they call and challenge us to a new affirmation of the body of Christ as God's vehicle for ministry in this world.

Moving toward Community

The question as to why I am a Christian is very different from the question of why, for example, I choose to live where I do. Where I live refers only to a specific aspect of my life and is set within a context of similar questions of existence: my job, my children's schools, the style of architecture I prefer.

By many hands the work of God is done.
—Richard Le Gallienne

But my Christian faith is not simply one aspect of my existence coequal with many others. Instead, it is the determining factor of who I am. I am a Christian because my identity has been forever and totally altered by personal encounter with Jesus Christ. All other areas of who I am are subsumed under the one category "Christian."

Churchmanship, for me, is a difficult part of that identity. The church itself is not immediately attractive to me. My natural inclination is to go my own way and to do my own thing. If I cannot run the show, I usually do not want to have any part of it.

But that is simply not the picture of New Testament Christianity. To be sure, the New Testament does not destroy individual freedom and decision making, nor does it suggest a mentality of a collective. At the same time, however, I simply cannot find in the early church a mention of a "Lone Ranger" Christianity. The church forever and always has been seen as a body, a community of faith, interrelating, interdependent, and intersubmissive.

To be sure, faith must be personal conviction and must be personally experienced, but Christian faith is genuinely found only within the context of community, a community that forms the types of relationships to which Christ calls us. No matter how much I might desire to do so, I cannot separate my faith from the context of community. It was within the community that I first experienced the nurture of Christian love, that the gospel was first presented, that I met Christ as Savior, and that I matured in the faith. In a very real sense, there is no Christian experience apart from the church.

And so I am left with the realization that my desire for independence in the faith cannot be a desire born of God. Instead, it is a product of self-centeredness, pride, and power mongering. It is a desire to establish my own kingdom which is accountable to no one beyond myself. It is not of God.

Ministry within the Body of Christ

There can be no doubt that the New Testament, especially the Pauline letters, gives men a great deal of spiritual authority within the context of the church. It is very important, though, that we understand that such authority *is spiritual* and *is within the context of the church.* Some men recognize the New Testament edict for a communal Christianity but carry a mentality of the corporation into the community of faith. They then claim that the spiritual authority given to men in the New Testament means that they ought to get to run the show. The result is an autocratic, hierarchical church that speaks nothing of community. The very concept of the communal identity of the church means that there must be an absolute sharing of responsibility within the walls of faith. The church can have but one head, and that must be Christ.

■ _____

The kingdom of God does not exist because of your effort or mine. It exists because God reigns. Our part is to enter this kingdom and bring our life under his sovereign will. —T. Z. Koo

_____ ■

So why all of the talk about the role of men in the New Testament church? I believe Paul was addressing a very real life situation at that time—one, incidentally, that has not changed all that much today. It seems that, from its inception, the church was more immediately attractive to women than it was to men. Women in that day and time were accustomed to submission—both mutual and outright. They understood the nature of communal living. For many of them, daily life was a time of degradation, humiliation, and debasement. The church set them free from that life. Its fellowship proclaimed their worthiness. It recognized them not as chattel but as God's creation, for whom Christ had died and for whom he had an eternal plan. The church was all about *freedom* for them.

Conversely, the church—on the surface—seemed to offer very little to men. Why would a man be attracted to the church in New Testament times? Unless he was a slave, he was ruler of his own world, master of his own fate. He carried absolute and unquestioned authority in his home. Acceptance into the church meant a surrender of power.

Paul's answer to those who questioned the value of the church for men is quite striking. He tells the men of that day that they have missed the point, that the struggles of this life are not about wealth, power, or control of the material. Instead, our battle is ". . . against principalities, against powers, against the rulers of the darkness of this age, against spiritual hosts of wickedness in the heavenly places." So, Paul's answer to the men of that day is, to paraphrase, "you may think you're winning, but you've got it all wrong. By giving up your authority and surrendering your will to Christ, you gain real authority. *Spiritual* authority. You are given the power to fight the genuinely important battles."

The basic difference between physical power and spiritual power is that men use physical power but spiritual power uses men. —Justin W. Nixon

---

How far have we progressed since New Testament times? Have we as men forgotten about the really important battles in life? Have we forgotten that there is life beyond the boardroom? When all of the children's Sunday school classes are taught exclusively by women, does that not say to young boys that the crucial matters of life, and especially of manhood, are not resolved within the context of the church? When Mom takes the kids to church while Dad stays home, doesn't that plant a seed of anticipation in a young man, looking forward to the day when he will outgrow the church?

There is no doubt—from Scripture or from experience—that God blesses the efforts of men who have committed themselves to the church. Whether a Timothy or a Martin Luther, a John Calvin or a John Stott, the story of the churchmen is a story of changed lives and victorious communities.

The Re-creation of Ministry

The New Testament is replete with metaphors for the church. It was called the bride of Christ, the people of God, the fellowship of faith. All of these metaphors are used to illustrate a certain role or function which the church fulfills.

I have a personal favorite, and it is the most common metaphor for the church in the New Testament. We are to be the body of Christ. On a simple basis, the body of Christ implies two things. First of all, it talks about a relationship, that we are all bound together as a body, a functioning unit under the headship of Christ. That tells us that we as individual Christians have an ultimate identity within the context of the body itself. We do not exist alone as an arm, a finger, or a leg. We exist because we are bound together.

The real intent of this metaphor, however, seems to be an explanation of a functional identity. That is, we not only relate as a body; we function as a body. We are, as the church of Jesus Christ, called to re-create the ministry of Jesus Christ.

In the twelfth chapter of 1 Corinthians, Paul gives explicit analysis of how we as the body function to bring about this ministry. In these verses, Paul was dealing with a specific and problematic situation in the church at Corinth. The members had claimed their spiritual authority, and God had blessed them with a profusion of gifts in order to birth the ministry of Christ among the membership and in the community surrounding the church. No church had more potential to change its world than did the church at Corinth.

Jesus deliberately turned his back on all the ideas of power held in the world and proposed something new: servanthood. —Arthur Adams

Instead of recognizing their unity as a functioning body, however, the church at Corinth began to seek authority not of the Spirit, but authority over one another. They began to claim that one gift was more important than another gift in order to establish a hierarchy of importance in the church.

Paul's response to them was that they did not understand the relationship brought about by the oneness of the Holy

Spirit, as the source of all gifts, and the oneness of the church, as the community in which the gifts were to be exercised. Paul emphasized to the church at Corinth that the gifts were not given for private edification, but for the sake of the common good. The members were given stewardship, not ownership, of the gifts, and they were always to be used for the benefit of the body. Paul constantly turned the attention away from the autonomy of the individual believer, from the authority of the individual believer, and returned that focus to the unity of the fellowship and the work of the church.

The greatest thing that could happen to our world today would be for men of God to determine to claim mutual authority in the church. Not the authority of hierarchy, lordship, or ruling, but the authority to exercise spiritual gifts and become a part of the functioning body of Christ. The problem in the church has never been lack of resources. It has forever been the unwillingness of the men of God to act as men of God.

Instead, we too often turn our attention toward those battles that are of secondary importance. We become consumed by the drive for power in relationship instead of by the desire for spiritual authority. If we have genuinely been called to be a part of a new order, then we cannot be driven by the concerns of the old. More and more, men are recognizing where the conflict really lies.

It is exciting to look around our nation and our world and see men who are taking their spiritual authority seriously. Men who have committed themselves to be Sunday school teachers or pastor-servants. Men who have taken seriously the call to address any task for which the church needs them. Men who have made their own agenda subservient to the call of the body.

The church is her true self only when she exists for humanity. —Dietrich Bonhoeffer

If we turn on our television sets, we cannot help but know that our world has more than its share of problems. Constant war, famine, and crime plague humankind. But most of the problems we see are but symptomatic of a deeper ill. Our world has a soul sickness, and all of the government initiatives, all the social programs, are but Band-Aids for gaping wounds. Our world changes only when we recognize the real source of conflict. No, our battle is not against the things of this world; it is against the principalities and the powers that debilitate and corrode the soul. We make a difference in this world as men of God only when we claim the power and authority promised to the church by Jesus Christ.

Playing with a Different Goal in Mind

BILL McCARTNEY
Former Head Football Coach,
University of Colorado

Colorado football and winning have been synonymous terms for a decade now. Inheriting a program near the bottom of the Big Eight, Coach Bill McCartney built the Buffaloes into a perennial national power. But coaching has never taken Coach McCartney away from his first love.

A few years ago, Coach McCartney was riding with Dr. Dave Wardell to address a Fellowship of Christian Athletes group in Pueblo, Colorado. While traveling, Coach McCartney and Dr. Wardell began praying and talking about their sense of ministry. Coach McCartney posed a question to Dr. Wardell: "If you could do anything at all in life, what would you do?" Dr. Wardell's response was immediate: "Disciple men." Coach McCartney then responded that his heart's desire was "to see men come together in the name of Jesus of Nazareth." As they continued their trip, the germ of an idea began to grow—an idea which has become a national Christian men's organization that we know as Promise Keepers.

Coach McCartney and Dr. Wardell realized that they were in a unique situation to provide a special ministry to the men of America. Men involved in athletics have a venue open to them that is not present for the population at large. They are accepted in any denomination and by the nonbelieving world as well. That open door needed to be used as an opportunity for ministry.

With a genuine sense of calling toward a national men's ministry, Coach McCartney and Dr. Wardell began to lay an ideological framework for what they wanted to accomplish. Both of them brought to the discussion a deep conviction. Coach McCartney recalls their early conversation: "It had been our experience that when just men were present and seeking God, we saw a great outpouring of the Holy Spirit. We wanted a ministry that talked about what it meant to be real men—men of fiber, substance, and conviction, but always men with a spiritual dimension. There is a very real sense in which we are proclaiming our destiny. We are making a statement of the brotherhood of men in America."

In May 1990, Coach McCartney and Dr. Wardell called a group of godly men together in a church to fast and pray. That was the genesis of Promise Keepers. The next year, over 22,000 men met on a basketball court with a genuine sense of proclaiming the lordship of Jesus Christ. By 1993, the group had grown to 50,000, and they moved the program to a football stadium. The next year, 1994, saw the genuine explosion of Promise Keepers. All across America men came together to revere the name of Jesus Christ. Over 37,000 men gathered for a meeting in Denton, Texas. In Portland, Oregon, the arena would only hold 30,000, and men had to be turned away. In Boulder, Colorado, 50,000 men came together for a service of praise and commitment. By the summer of 1994, Promise Keepers had ninety full-time employees, and a ministry to hundreds of thousands.

One of the key terms for Promise Keepers is accountability. Coach McCartney feels that in the last half of the twentieth century, we have so watered down the message of Jesus Christ that it has little impact on our culture. A whole new generation of men is not convinced of the validity or the practicality of the message of Jesus Christ. When men come together in a situation where they are held accountable to each other, however, it changes their sense of responsibility toward each other. "One man always raises the standard for another man. When I see a man on his knees, it drives me to my knees. I'm held accountable not only by his attitude, but also by his action. When one man turns to another man and asks, 'In the name of Jesus, how is your marriage?' there is no room for an answer of compromise. It requires us to be truthful and honest about our responsibility before God.

"It is within the sense of fellowship and the sense of bonding that we are set free to distribute what we have received. In the Holy Land there are two bodies of water, both on the Jordan River and not very far apart. One is dead, lifeless, and pollutes everything it touches; it is known as the Dead Sea. A little ways upstream is a beautiful, living, thriving body of water which some people say is one of the most pristine lakes on earth; it is the Sea of Galilee. The difference in the two? No water flows out of the Dead Sea. It only takes in. On the other hand, the Sea of Galilee puts out as much as it receives. Its life is a result of the fact that it distributes.

"In the same way, men who only take from the church, who only take from life, are spiritually dead. We are called on to distribute, to pass on to other men all that Jesus has given us."

What's in store for Promise Keepers? The summer of 1995 will be a focal time. Coach McCartney expects one million men to be in Washington, D.C., not at a political rally, not to protest for or against U.S. policies, but to ask forgiveness from God for "dropping the ball as men." In the truest sense of the word, Coach McCartney is calling upon the men of America to be faithful to the divine commission in their churches, homes, and workplaces.

MAINTAINING PERSPECTIVE: CHRISTIAN DISCIPLINES IN THE MARKETPLACE

11

> The desperate need today is not for a greater
> number of intelligent people, or gifted people,
> but for deep people.
> Richard Foster

I would meet you for breakfast," my friend said, "but I'm going to a Bible study in the morning. Why don't you join me?" At 6:30 the next morning, I joined him and a group of other men for a time of Bible study and prayer. My experience that morning was one that is repeated throughout the United States, indeed, throughout the world, almost every day. Among the men gathered there that morning were the corporate elite of their city. The CEOs of three separate petroleum concerns sat among the group. The president of a regional medical center was there as were a prominent surgeon and several attorneys.

Was this their secret of corporate success? Had they found a new and better method for doing business? Not really, but what they had done was tap into one of the genuine sources of inner power and peace that has been known for centuries. Especially in Christian corporate America, there has been, over the last few years, a rediscovery of the spiritual disciplines and of the change that they can bring in our lives.

The business world is a place of hurry, a place of bustle and pressure. It is easy to lose track of the important things in life. Without the sense of peace and ordering that the spiritual disciplines bring to our lives, it becomes very difficult to maintain a Christian perspective as we go about our daily tasks. But such a perspective is requisite for the believer. When we begin to look at the New Testament, the case for Christianity is a case for a pervasive influence in all of our lives.

The life of the New Testament believer is never divided into secular and sacred realms. Instead, the faith of the child of God permeates all that is done. It is especially important to note that the spiritual disciplines of prayer, meditation, Bible study, and fasting are never compartmentalized. Instead, they are incorporated into the daily life of the believer.

Many believers today are rediscovering the ancient truth of the all-encompassing nature of our faith. Paul encourages us to always maintain a spirit of prayer. We are also reminded to think on those things that are pure and those things that are worthwhile. Jesus himself set the example of fasting, prayer, and meditation for us. The story of Christianity cannot be told without a recounting of the role of the spiritual disciplines.

Toward a Normative Christianity

When we look at the Christian faith, we often divide its practice into that which is the standard for normal folks, and that which is characteristic of the super Christian. For the average believer, faith can usually be no more than a marginal part of life. We attend church on Sunday, we have a regular prayer time, and we want to raise our children in general agreement with Christian principles. But, it stops at that point. Our faith does not constantly press itself down upon our consciousness, always involved and always a part of who we are. That kind of faith is reserved for the stars among the saints.

I once heard a Bible study leader describe the Beatitudes as "a prescription for super Christianity." I strongly disagree. The New Testament knows nothing of a super Christianity. It knows only normative Christianity, a system of faith and belief that demands preeminence in the lives of all of its followers— not just those who have gained notoriety as the superstars of the practice.

And so it is with spiritual disciplines. They are not the special province of the gifted and talented of the faith. Instead, they are an integral part of the experience and practice of New Testament Christianity.

Many Christians get very uneasy when talk shifts to the subject of the spiritual disciplines. Prayer may be a part of our lives, but it is probably not constantly present. Meditation usually sounds a little bit too New Age for us to find comfort in it. And fasting—don't even think about fasting. It serves no purpose in the modern world unless you are trying to lose weight.

Prayer, meditation, Bible study, and fasting are known as the classic Christian disciplines. Classic in the sense that they are timeless expressions of faith. And, for countless believers through the centuries, the disciplines have been the means to a deeper faith and clearer relationship.

A Different Focus

I like things that are black and white. I like well-constructed syllogisms, hard-and-fast rules, and rational explanations. In fact, most men with whom I come into contact feel the same. There is a discomfort, an ill-at-easeness, when we sense that someone is getting mystical on us.

Yet, at the same time, I yearn for something deeper in my life. I want to experience God not just in some logical construct, but in the reality of his existence, with an awareness of his presence that overwhelms me and drives me to my knees. I want to *know* God.

The spiritual disciplines are all about a normative Christianity that genuinely experiences God. They are not an invitation to some foggy mysticism in which the answers to the challenges of our lives appear to us out of a misty nowhere. Instead, they bring an awareness of the deeper truths of life, and a consciousness of the ministry of the Spirit of God to each one of us. The spiritual disciplines are about fine-tuning our hearts, our minds, the whole of our existence, to the voice of God and to his activity in our lives.

Specifically, this faith relationship with God permeates the whole of our existence. The spiritual disciplines are intended to be part of the life of every Christian. This is not a super spirituality reserved for the giants of the church, beyond the reach of the Everyman of faith. Not at all. God gave us spiritual disciplines to serve as guideposts of spiritual life for all believers. The spiritual disciplines are to be practiced by adults and children, by men and women, by the rich and the poor, by all who walk in faith.

The disciplines are not to be dichotomized from our daily lives. Because our faith is a permeating faith, they are to be practiced in the midst of everything we do. We take the disciplines to the office with us in the morning; we take them home with us in the evening. They become a part of who we are.

Nor should we consider the disciplines hard-driving taskmasters. They are not a gift of God designed to drive all joy from our existence. Instead, the spiritual disciplines are the path to freedom. In a world that is captured by self-interest, materialism, driven competitiveness, and insecurity, the disciplines are often a pathway to an awareness of the reality of God in our lives—an awareness that sets us free from the drudgery and the pain of the day-to-day. *The spiritual disciplines are about joy.*

This is not to say, however, that the spiritual disciplines are an easy path to Christian wholeness. After all, they are *disciplines*. They require diligence, patience, and application. But within our efforts, we experience God's grace.

The Transforming Power of the Disciplines

Scripture uses many terms to describe sin. One word that is used pictures sin as a missing of the mark. Another term suggests that sin is a falling short of a goal. In still another place, sin is pictured as an act of rebellion against a righteous and holy God. The problem of sin is prevalent enough to merit all of these metaphors.

For the most part, when we think of sin, we think of specific acts and, according to the biblical image, that is certainly part of the definition. But it is only a part. In the larger biblical picture, sin is less what we do than it is who we are. Paul speaks of the struggle against flesh, the attempt to control who he is when it seems there is a pernicious and pervasive desire to live in rebellion.

For most of us who live in a world of black and white, it is much easier to deal with sin as activity than it is with sin as condition. If it is wrong to do something, we simply need to stop doing it. If it is right to do something else, we need to start doing it. Yet somehow sin seems to keep creeping back into my life, and all my resolve does not seem to act as a barrier against it.

The father of the Reformation, the monk Martin Luther, wrestled with the same problem. Consumed by a desire to do what was right yet still unable to control his flesh, he regularly scourged himself—beat himself with a lash—attempting to bring his body into submission and into submission of his will to do right. But he still found that he failed miserably. What Martin Luther discovered at a later day in his life was that the world of God's grace is a world of freedom, with a promise of escaping the clutches of sin.

The spiritual disciplines are not a shortcut to purity; they are not the easy route to freedom from sin. But they certainly are a part of the pathway. The easy road to righteousness has not yet been given us. In fact, the term *easy* will probably always cancel out the idea of righteousness just as *cheap* contradicts the idea of grace.

But nonetheless, meditation, fasting, prayer, and Bible study are the means by which we find dependence upon God, a dependence that leads to the holier and purer walk that brings more and more freedom from sinfulness.

In 1979, I walked through a Christian bookstore in Houston, Texas. In the section containing titles on prayer and spiritual growth, I picked up a book by an author named Richard Foster. Its title was *Celebration of Discipline*. Over the next few weeks I was introduced to the concept of the spiritual disciplines in the life of the believer. Along with thousands and thousands of other Christians, I discovered a missing element of my faith— a transforming element of my faith. In a very brief form over the next few pages, we will touch on the spiritual disciplines, and the power to change our lives. It is my prayer that the journey to the disciplines is a journey that will last you a lifetime.

Meditation

Our clocks seem to run faster today than they did ten years ago. I recently made a trip with the president of a major corporation. Our mornings started with breakfast at 6:30, and our business days often did not conclude until after midnight. One morning, in the midst of our breakfast coffee, he remarked to me, "I simply don't know how any executive can get everything done in eight hours. A ten- or twelve-hour day simply does not give me enough time to accomplish all I have to do."

And so it is across America. Corporate executives go at full speed for eight, ten, and twelve hours a day. Business offices are not quiet, sterile places, but virtual hives of activity. American business is all about doing.

Yet there is something forever superficial about doing. It may be activity with a purpose, to be sure, but its hurries and demands do nothing to bring us inner peace and control. On the contrary, we are driven to distraction, and turmoil rages inside of us.

> *True contemplation is not a psychological trick but a theological grace.* —Thomas Merton

We live in a culture that rewards shallowness. This seems to be as true for the church as it is for any other institution. We look for a quick-fix religion that demands nothing from us. We equate spiritual depth more with charts which outline the time of Christ's return than we do with self-sacrifice and spiritual responsibility. We are more interested in feeling good on Sunday morning than we are in humbling ourselves before the altar of Christ.

In the midst of a culture that constantly calls us to superficiality and shallowness, the discipline of meditation is a clarion call back to inner peace and inner wholeness before God. Christian meditation is not an arena reserved for New Age wackos. It is, in the words of Thomas Merton, "a theological grace," a gift of God with a long history both in Scripture and in Christian writings.

While New Age and Eastern religions stress meditation as a way to separate ourselves from the world, the Christian concept of meditation is one of immersing ourselves in God's creation as part of his redemptive action. Merton wrote, "Meditation has no point and no reality unless it is firmly rooted in life."

The Bible abounds with references to meditation. We are told that Isaac "went out to meditate in the field in the evening" (Gen. 24:63). In God's commission to Joshua as he became the leader of the children of Israel was the direction, "Do not let this Book of the Law depart from your mouth; meditate on it day and night" (Josh. 1:8 NIV). Psalm 119 could be called the Song of Meditation because it continually recounts the joy of spiritual reflection.

Meditation is definitely scriptural, but how do we go about doing it? You will find the answer neither in Scripture nor in this book. We simply do not have a little instruction manual for meditation. There are, however, some practical pointers that should be considered when meditating.

Meditation is the opening of our minds, our hearts, and our spirits to the ministering of God through his Holy Spirit. Throughout our lives, there should be both a sense of meditation and an act of meditation. We have a sense of meditation when we develop a constant attentiveness to the working of God in our lives. We are called upon to be spiritually aware. As Paul instructs us to "pray without ceasing," we are also to meditate without ceasing. We are to live a lifestyle that continually seeks to hear God.

But a lifestyle of meditation is impossible to maintain without a specific time of dedicated meditation. That is, we need to set aside a time daily for quiet contemplation before God. This must be a time when we free ourselves from the distractions of the everyday. No television, no radio blaring in the background, but a time of genuine withdrawal into the presence of God.

Beyond such a basic description, however, there is no way to tell someone how to meditate. The good news, however, is that there is not a secret formula that we have to discover before we can enter into the presence of God. What God earnestly desires for us is fellowship and communion with him. Therefore, when we draw ourselves away from the cares of the day and open ourselves up to the ministry of his Spirit, he is there to touch us, to cleanse, to purify.

While there are few explicit instructions, we can see a pattern of meditation in Scripture. God commands Joshua to meditate on the Book of the Law. The psalmist often speaks of meditat-

> *What we do with our lives outwardly, how well we care for others, is as much a part of meditation as what we do in the quietness and turning inward. In fact, Christian meditation that does not make a difference in the quality of one's outer life is short-circuited. It may flare for awhile, but unless it results in finding richer and more loving relationships with other human beings or in changing conditions in the world that cause human suffering, the chances are that an individual's prayer activity will fizzle out.*   —Morton Kelsey

ing upon the Word of God. The psalmist also speaks regularly of meditation upon the goodness of God as revealed in his creation and in his graciousness. So we are at least presented a biblical model of meditation. As we set aside a time of contemplation before God, we can reflect upon the Word of God, both as it reveals him to us and convicts of sin. We can also spend time meditating upon the goodness and the greatness of God. As we are faithful to set aside time to be quiet and still before a loving and gracious Father, the Bible teaches that God will minister to us and pull us into a deeper relationship.

Prayer

Man's concept of time and pace has changed through the decades. We live in a compressed world where everything must be done faster and quicker than it was in the time of our parents and certainly in the days of our grandparents. A few years ago I picked up a book by the great English pastor Charles Spurgeon. In one section of the book entitled "Private and Public Prayer," Spurgeon discussed the amount of time that should be devoted by believers both in their private prayer and in their public praying. "Our prayers should not be long and tedious," Spurgeon wrote, "especially our public ones. We should give great care to see that our public prayers are brief and to the point." That advice made sense to me. We've all been in those places where the public prayer dragged on not for thirty seconds or for a minute, but for five and even ten minutes—a time which can seem like an eternity in such a situation. I then read on. "No," Spurgeon said, "a public prayer should not run on. It should be much shorter than our private time of prayer. In fact," he said, "a public prayer should probably never last longer than fifteen minutes." *Fifteen minutes?* Is it our attitude toward *time* or our attitude toward *prayer* that has changed so much in the intervening years?

No practice is more central to the Christian idea of piety than is prayer. William Carey affirmed the position of prayer for all believers: "Prayer—secret, fervent, believing prayer—lies at the root of all personal godliness." Through the ages, prayer has been the hallmark of the great spiritual battle, the trumpet call to Christian service, and the refuge of those in desperate need of divine intervention. It forms the center of the Christian life. It constitutes the essence of our speaking to God and awaiting his answer.

When we look at the lives of the heroes of the faith, both those from Scripture and those who have appeared in the chapters of history written since New Testament time, we find that the story of the vital life of the church is the story of prayer. Even in a casual reading of the Psalms, we find David continually falling upon his face before God, crying out, "How long, oh Lord?" The central act of relationship for Jesus' life was the time he spent in prayer. The story of the temptation following the period of forty days of fasting and prayer and the great grief of the garden prayer are the life of Jesus in microcosm. Peter, Paul, James, and John constantly called the early church to prayer.

Martin Luther was so consumed by the necessity of prayer that he stated, "I have so much business I cannot get on without spending three hours daily in prayer." Wesley, Spurgeon, Edwards, Graham, and Stott have all written and spoken of the necessity of dedicated prayer time in their own spiritual journeys.

And this central role of prayer is not just reserved for the lives of "professional" Christians. When I think of those men in whose lives I most see a spirit of Christian wisdom and peace, my thoughts are always of men who have made a consistent commitment to prayer. Men like Harry Congdon, a commercial artist, whose prayer list always sits beside his chair in his living room waiting for him to come in each morning. Men like Henry Langford, a central Texas rancher, who rises each morning and drives out into his pasture to park and spend time alone with God. Famous Christians? No. Heroes of the faith? Most certainly.

As often as not, however, we are defeated rather than challenged when we look at those who have progressed far in the journey of prayer. Fifteen minutes of time before the Lord each day seems like an almost insurmountable task, not even to consider a daily hour or two. Even our feeble efforts seem to fall flat. We make a commitment to really spend that earnest time before God, but quickly give up when we find ourselves failing to reach a prescribed minimal limit on our knees.

But learning to pray is a process. As the athlete trains to build endurance and expertise, so do we recognize that our prayer life can grow through the time, the effort, and the faithfulness with which we approach it.

Prayer is a grace, to be sure. But just as we learn to experience the grace of God's love by becoming more familiar with his presence and more aware of his speaking to us, so do we learn to experience the grace of prayer.

■ ─────────────────────────────

Prayer is exhaling the spirit of man and inhaling the Spirit of God.　　　　　—Edwin Keith

───────────────────────────── ■

The apostles asked Jesus, "Teach us to pray." Understanding that prayer is a learning process sets us free to experiment, to fail, and to grow. There is no room in this chapter for an exhaustive discussion of the nature and the importance of prayer in the life of the Christian. Many great classics on the subject of prayer have been written by those far more advanced in the practice.

There is one area of prayer, however, that is so integral to the entire understanding of the Christian disciplines that it demands some mention here. The act of confession of our sinfulness before God paves the way for ongoing spiritual renewal in our lives, yet so often we dedicate little of our prayer time and effort to the acknowledgment of our sins, seeking forgiveness for those transgressions. Confessing sin opens our lives to God's forgiving grace and allows us to experience the fullness and the richness of his love.

It should be remembered, however, that even the act of confession takes place within the context of God's grace. Sometimes we are so hardened and calloused by the sinfulness that seems to be a part of our lives that we are not even aware of the depths of our sin. If you really are serious about righteousness, if you really want to know God in a deeper way, then begin your prayers with "Oh, Lord, show to me my sinfulness." When we catch a glimpse of how very far we are from the standard that God has placed before us, it can do nothing but drive us to his mercy and to dependence upon his provision. Within the grace of confession, we find the experience of God's love for us. And then we confess with Paul, "While we were yet sinners, Christ died for us."

Fasting

Nothing is further from the sensibilities of the twentieth-century, first-world Christian than is the practice of fasting. The whole concept of fasting, with its demands of self-denial, its air of mysticism, and its seeming pretense of piety, does not sit well with the contemporary expressions of propositional Christianity. It is a practice that seems of little importance to today's Christian.

Yet it is an extremely biblical practice. We find Jesus in the wilderness, fasting and seeking guidance from the Father. We find the writers throughout the New Testament speaking of setting time aside for fasting and prayer. And Jesus implicitly commands it. He says to his followers, "When you fast, do not be like the hypocrites, with a sad countenance." Notice that Jesus very consciously uses the term *when* rather than the term *if.* The assumption for him clearly was that the believer would spend time fasting.

Yes, fasting is about as biblical as a believer can get. But, as with meditation, the Bible gives us precious little information about the why of fasting. Let me suggest that there are three primary ways in which fasting aids us as a spiritual discipline. First, it moves us away from concern about our own physical well-being. On the whole, Americans are consumed by consumption. Our entire focus is on what we bring in for ourselves and how we meet our own needs. Believers who would never consider telling a lie nor entering into sexual promiscuity may feel no guilt about gluttony. Fasting gets us off of the race track of consumption and attention to our physical needs. It helps us to understand that we can do without. It helps us to see that the whole focus of our existence does not have to be on providing physical needs.

Second, and this is really the other side of the same coin, fasting turns our attention toward God. It is, to be sure, very possible to fast without ever thinking of God. If, however, we go into our time of fasting earnestly and honestly seeking God's presence, our preoccupation on provision of our physical needs is set aside, and we can fully focus on our relationship with God.

Finally, and this very well may be the most important aspect, fasting makes a statement to us about the seriousness of the maintenance of spiritual relationships, and a statement to

God about our seriousness in maintaining those relationships. Anyone can talk a good Christianity. We can profess our seriousness and proclaim our righteousness. Fasting is not talk; it is activity. Fasting requires effort and commitment. Fasting has never been about fashionable or easy Christianity. It is about a genuine, heartfelt and body-enacted commitment to spiritual growth. God sees such resolve and rewards it.

Serious fasting cannot be for every Christian. My father had a deep and abiding relationship with the Spirit of God, yet fasting was never a possibility for him. During almost all of the years I knew him, his body was assaulted by heart disease. To fast was a physical impossibility. There are those, certainly, who should never enter into a program of fasting because of health concerns.

But for most of us, fasting can bring significant physical benefits as well as spiritual blessings. Just as in prayer or meditation, however, we have to learn to fast. An excellent starting point is to have a one-day-a-week, twenty-four-hour fast. Such a fast would entail going from lunch to lunch without eating, meaning that two meals would be missed. Most adults in sound health could endure such a fast with little negative effect.

When a time is set aside for fasting, we are instructed by Christ not to make too big a deal out of it. In other words, we do not wear our piety on our sleeves. A fast should be a very private thing. It may be known to your family or a close friend, but it is not something that is broadcast throughout our offices or our neighborhoods. Instead, it is a time when we very quietly and very comfortably begin to focus our attention back on our relationship with Christ.

You may be very surprised to discover how much of your time is devoted to the preparation and eating of meals. Fasting frees that time to be used for prayer, meditation, and Bible study. It allows us to focus on the development of our spiritual relationships. As we learn to fast, the first inclination is to focus on the physical aspects of the food deprivation. We think about food, how we feel about food, and we wonder if we will be able to make it to the end of the fast. But as we progress and learn to incorporate this as a regular part of our spiritual discipline, the fast can become a time which is eagerly anticipated, a time of spiritual renewal, and a time for setting aside material needs in order to focus on spiritual growth.

For many individuals, the ending of the fast is a time in which the presence of God is experienced in a very real and a very significant way. To some extent, this is a time of re-engaging the world. It is a time when we are reminded that our spiritual needs and the reality of the physical world are not that far apart. It is a time when we can gain a new commitment to walking with Christ and to letting each day be a time of experiencing his grace.

As Charles Wesley wrote, "It was not merely by the light of reason that the people of God have been directed to use fasting, but they have been taught of it of God himself by clear and open revelations of his will. Now, whatever reasons there were to quicken those of old in the zealous and constant discharge of this duty, they are of equal force still to quicken us."

The Discipline of Study

When I was in college, I worked with a group of young people at a church in Houston, Texas. During that time and in the years since, I have had the opportunity to watch many of that same group progress through their teenage years and into adulthood. It seems to me that there is a clear separation in how those teenagers turned out. Some of them, from the standpoint of spiritual evaluation, have not seen a lot of success. Others have grown to be outstanding Christian men and women. They are leaders in their communities, in their businesses, in their homes, and in their churches.

When I look at that group and ask why one turned out one way or one went a different road, I always come back to the same conclusion. One factor ultimately makes a difference: Bible study. There were, undoubtedly, many influences on the lives of these young Christians. There were different home situations, different personalities, and different levels of commitment from the beginning. But the ones who are the church leaders today are the ones who made a commitment to Bible study during their teenage years.

Unfortunately, today the Bible is less a true guide to life and living than it is a club with which to batter those who do not share our approach to the faith. The debate in the evangelical community about the nature of Scripture is entirely misplaced. While there is no doubt that the integrity of Scripture is of critical importance for all believers, it certainly seems that we spend more time arguing about the nature of God's Word than we spend immersed in Scripture. The debate over the Bible which has polarized contemporary evangelicalism is by and large political and self-serving in nature—and of little purpose for either the believer or the church.

> *Our Bible is not an amulet, a magical charm, but a book to be read, marked, inwardly digested and translated into life.*
> —J. Philip Hyatt

What is beyond dispute is that we are called by Scripture to bury ourselves in it, to become so familiar with it that it becomes a part of living. The Bible is very clear that the Word of God is a transforming power, that these are not simply words on a page, but indeed that God himself is active in his Word.

In a very real sense, the study of Scripture becomes a culmination of all of the inner spiritual disciplines. Scripture is the foundation upon which we build our spiritual lives. What separates the Christian tradition of fasting, meditation, and prayer from Eastern mysticism or New Age religiosity? Scripture does. A New Age adherent may speak of hearing the voice of God and affirming the sanctity of self, but immersion in Scripture allows "a measuring of the spirits." A daily program of Bible study constantly calls us back to the reality of the claims of Jesus Christ and gives us the standard against which to measure all claims of spirituality. It opens the door for the working of Christ, and speaks to us as only God's Word can.

When we read the stories of the saints from New Testament times to the present age, we read the lives of those who are intimately connected with the Word of God. The Protestant Reformation began when Martin Luther "discovered the strange, new world of the New Testament." It was in returning to Scripture that Karl Barth rejected nineteenth-century liberalism and discovered "the word of the living God." And each day and in each age we discover anew the power of Scripture to transform our lives and to call us into deeper and more meaningful relationship.

Putting It All Together

This chapter was never intended to be an exhaustive compendium of the spiritual disciplines. Many of our guides to Christian life would take us beyond the four disciplines listed here and include other areas such as submission, solitude, service, and worship. Even for the topics discussed in this chapter, much more exhaustive treatments have been offered by those deeply skilled in their practice.

But this is a starting point. It is an introduction to a way of life that has profoundly shaped those who have walked closely to the presence of our Lord. The discipline of Christian faith is that which permeates and alters all that we are. Let this chapter be the beginning of a lifelong journey.

12

EXTENDING THE FAMILY: A WITNESS IN THE OFFICE AND AT HOME

Evangelism is the struggle for the salvation of this world.
D. T. Niles

New life is not created in and of itself. Despite scientific breakthroughs and Huxleyan predictions, a child can be conceived only through the contributions of both a man and a woman. And may it ever stay that way.

Much in the same manner, God has chosen to share the creation of new spiritual life with us. I have heard of those individuals who, seemingly without input from any other person, became Christians. I have heard of them, but never met one. In the vast majority of cases, it is through the active participation of another individual—or often a group of individuals—that someone comes to know Jesus Christ as Savior. I would suspect that for even most of those who claim a Damascus Road experience, in which it appears that no one else is involved, back there somewhere there was someone who modeled Christ or at least opened the door to faith for them.

That is simply the way God works. The pattern of Scripture is very consistent. The followers of God are constantly and consistently called upon to participate with him in all of his activities.

A Theology of Evangelism

In the New Testament, we find the story of God's second grand adventure. The first enterprise was, of course, the forming of human life and the world around it. As we have discussed throughout this book, after the initiation of that first work, God then called upon humankind to join him in the endeavor of creation and dominion. That was our initial calling.

The New Testament is a record of God's creation of a new order, a new world, if you will. Paul says, "Therefore, if anyone is in Christ, he is a new creation; old things have passed away; behold, all things have become new" (2 Cor. 5:17). It should by no means surprise us, then, that just as he did in the Old Testament, God calls upon us to join with him in this new enterprise. We are to become the agents of redemption by taking up the task that has come to be known as evangelism.

In a very real sense, the Old Testament serves as a guidebook for our partnership with God in the journey of creation and dominion. It specifically focuses on the details of that partnership—that is, how we are to relate to God both as our Lord and as the one who shares the task with us. The Ten Commandments are a wonderful recitation for the proper structure of that relationship and its maintenance as well as how we are to fulfill the demands of our commission.

The New Testament takes us to the next level of relationship and commission. It is not only the proclamation of the salvation in Jesus Christ; it is also our primer for sharing in the task of redemption. The Gospels and the beginning of the book of Acts bring to us the good news of Jesus Christ. The rest of Acts and the Epistles show how this new commission was worked out in the early church and set a pattern for us to emulate.

In no place is the commission given more clearly than it is in Matthew 28:19–20: "Go therefore and make disciples of all the nations, baptizing them in the name of the Father and of the Son and of the Holy Spirit, teaching them to observe all things that I have commanded you; and lo, I am with you always, even to the end of the age." Two parts really comprise this instruction, both of which fall into the general category of making disciples. The first part of our job, we are told, is to baptize in the name of the Father, the Son, and the Holy Spirit. This represents the calling of an individual to a repentant, saving knowledge of Jesus Christ. We usually call this task evangelism.

The New Testament is replete with instructions that we are to be about the business of evangelism. The act of bearing witness to the saving power of Jesus Christ can even be said to be the central, world-related activity of all the people of God. It is very much the starting point.

The second section of this commission stands alongside evangelism and completes the mission of redemption. To fulfill the commandment to make disciples, we must not only evangelize but must also teach them "to observe all things that I have commanded you." In other words, we not only bring people into the faith, but we also help them grow toward righteousness. In so doing, we complete the task of redemption.

I want to be very intentional in what I am communicating here: *I am not suggesting that the grace of Jesus Christ alone is insufficient to bring salvation, that good works have to be added on before a person can be considered saved.* What I am suggesting, however, is that salvation by grace is never pictured in the New Testament as something that exists in and of itself. It exists within the whole matrix of growing righteously toward God. The relationship is not a destination; it is a journey.

Professing, saving faith is always seen as the beginning of a process, the end of which is a righteous lifestyle in the individual who has been called into that saving faith. Paul himself said, ". . . work out your own salvation with fear and trembling," suggesting to us that he did not see his experience on the

Damascus Road or the following events in Jerusalem as an ultimate end. Rather, they were the beginning of a journey for him. We call this journey *sanctification*. Sanctification is a process by which we grow toward godliness.

Together, the calling of people to Christ and helping them grow to maturity in Christ make up the process of redemption. One cannot exist without the other. Individuals do not grow to become Christlike without first experiencing his grace. Likewise, acceptance of Jesus Christ as Savior places a demand of growth on the life of the individual. It is the greatest of heresy to suggest that Jesus could come into someone's life and it make absolutely no difference in their lifestyle. When we change identity, we change activity.

Our participation in each of these enterprises is not an optional activity. We do not have the choice of saying, "I will lead others to Christ, but I won't help them grow up." Nor may we choose only to be involved in the maturation of other Christians and leave the task of evangelism to those we believe to be more fit. By any measure of the New Testament edict, we are called upon to be active participants in the full process of redemption.

First Steps

One of the great disasters in contemporary American society is the large number of children who are starting families. The huge increase in the number of teenage parents has fearful consequences for the structure of our society as a whole—before we even consider what it does to their children. We recognize that the beginning of a family is not an undertaking to be entered lightly. Marriage and parenting is a serious business requiring both knowledge and the maturity to actuate that knowledge.

In like manner, neither would we suggest that an individual jump in without training and preparation and start a business. Starting a business is also a serious matter. Poorly prepared owners or managers almost always see a business fail.

But both starting a family and starting a business are ways of fulfilling what God has instructed us to do in the very first chapters of Genesis. Yet, we recognize that even if they are within the scope of divine will, there is a time, a place, and a procedure for each. On the other hand, we somehow think that because the gift of salvation has been brought to us, we are immediately ready and capable to make disciples. May I suggest that the issue is drawn in a little more complicated fashion than that? While we may have a story to tell, we ourselves must mature in the faith before we can direct others to maturity.

We need to begin with first steps. The tentative steps into the world of making disciples begin with modeling a lifestyle that is conducive to the spiritual birth and spiritual growth of all who observe you. In the early chapters of Acts, Luke gives us a description of how the early church related to one another: "And they continued steadfastly in the apostles' doctrine and fellowship, in the breaking of bread, and in prayers . . . praising God and having favor with all the people." Luke then goes on to record, "And the Lord added to the church daily those who were being saved." The point here is that Christians were conducting themselves in such a way that no one could find fault with them. Being found blameless, their lifestyle attracted those who saw them to relationship with Jesus Christ.

The lifestyle we display must be genuinely reflective of the work that Christ is conducting within us. When I was in college, I worked for a construction firm. One of our carpenters had been a Christian for a year or two, and he seemed to take the idea of making disciples quite seriously. Wherever he was on the job site, he had a radio playing (rather loudly) Christian music. He carried a New Testament in his pocket, conspicuously bowed his head in prayer before each lunch break, and had a "Praise the Lord!" for almost any situation he encountered. Unfortunately, his faith somehow never reached his work habits. He was habitually late, was a shoddy craftsman, and always seemed to run out of money before the end of the month. His witness (and he certainly had one) turned many more people away from the faith than were ever called to it by his example.

In the same company, there was another man, a brick mason. He also took the task of evangelism quite seriously. But, well, let's just say he did not wear his Christianity on his sleeve quite as much. What he did do was display a strong work ethic, had honesty and integrity in all of his dealings, and was open and willing to talk to anyone about Jesus Christ at any time. I could not help but notice that when anyone on the crew ran into difficult times in their lives, it was to this man that they turned for counsel and guidance.

In like manner, we are called upon by our task to live a lifestyle that beckons others toward a relationship with Jesus Christ. That is the beginning point. As we face the ethical dilemmas that are part and parcel of the business world, we are to show others what it means to be a Christian, to be faithful to the commands of Christ. We are to conduct ourselves in all our enterprises as those who have a genuine sense of responsibility toward the ethics of Christ.

Spreading the Word

It *is* very important that we live a life that calls others into relationship with Jesus Christ, but just living that lifestyle is not enough. That is where it begins, but we must go beyond. If we are maturing as Christians in the way that the Bible says we must, we also have an obligation to specifically lead others to a saving knowledge of Jesus Christ.

The excuse, "I let my life be a witness," is precisely that— an excuse to avoid being faithful to the commands of Scripture. The problem, you see, is that people are never led to Christ by example alone. Most certainly, an attractive and righteous lifestyle may be something that others see and want to emulate. Unless, however, it is explained that the lifestyle is the result of God's grace which is also available to them, then they will not experience the transforming power of Jesus Christ in their lives.

And so, we are called upon to bear witness, both with our actions and our words, of what God has done in our lives. It is not a terrible task to which God sends us. Rather, it is a joyous enterprise in which we join with God to fulfill his purposes in the world.

Witness in the Home

In no place does the task of redemption take on greater importance than it does in the home. Just as God did not create the world and then leave it in its fallen state to find redemption on its own, neither can we lose sight of the awesome task of leading our families to salvation and spiritual maturity. It might even be said that we are doubly commissioned when it comes to the point of our families; we have the obligation toward all people for the task of evangelism, and we have a special calling of ministry to our family members. So God calls us to this ministry at both points.

The process of salvation for children of the faithful seems immeasurably smoother and easier. Raised in a Christian home, I cannot remember a time when I did not know that God loves me. The affirmation of his lordship in my life was a natural culmination of my experiences with him in early childhood.

Many studies have demonstrated that the vast majority of church growth is organic. That is, most baptisms and church memberships come from the children of families already in the church. Many who study church growth argue that this means that the church is not accomplishing its mission of reaching a lost world. Let me suggest that those statistics could be read as a statement of affirmation that the message of Christ is being propagated in Christian families, as it should be.

When we practice a faith in the home where conversation and conduct reflect the living reality of Christ in our lives, the transition to faith for our children will be a natural part of their lives. The most important thing we can do for our children is to make faith a living reality. By so doing, we can invite them into life with Jesus Christ. Such is the greatest investment you will ever make for your family.

Faith in the Office

In one of the interviews for this book, I inadvertently used the term *Christian corporation*. The company president immediately responded, "Please don't call us a Christian corporation. We are a company. A corporation by its very nature cannot be Christian. That is not the purpose of the corporation. Neither does calling us a Christian corporation do justice to the name Christian." Point well made. I really don't see how a corporation *could* have leading people to a saving knowledge of Jesus Christ as its purpose.

This task of redemption is the ultimate calling that we can ever experience. William Temple was perhaps the greatest theologian to ever serve as Archbishop of Canterbury. His writings in natural theology shaped a whole generation of students. While still in his thirties, he assumed the mantle of a very important parish in London. One evening three of his Anglican colleagues came to him, requesting that he become the leader of a discipleship program throughout England. They felt that it was "time to go to the people with the gospel of Jesus. We think you are the man to lead it. We can offer you only half the salary you are getting. It might all be a mistake. Will you accept?"

After days of deliberation, Temple responded, "I am ready." The resulting renewal breathed fires of life into the long-stagnant Church of England. Temple's willingness to answer the call changed the lives of thousands.

At the same time, however, there is a place within the corporation for the sharing of the gospel of Jesus Christ. Or at least there used to be. With EEOC guidelines, company policies, and a secular society, there certainly are strictures on when and how we can share our faith at the office. And, when we are on company time, we have an obligation to live within the company policies.

We also have an obligation to witness to the work of Christ. If we are conducting ourselves in a manner that gives evidence of the grace of God in our lives, other people will notice, and the door for sharing our faith will be opened. Being a Christian *must* make a difference in the way we live. And that difference will be forever attractive to those with whom we come into contact.

As others begin to see that there is something different in our lives, the relationships that we have formed with co-workers and friends will provide the opportunity to tell them of the saving grace of Jesus Christ. But, we must be watchful for those opportunities that come and go without us ever noticing them. The especially sensitive Christian is the one constantly aware of the Holy Spirit's provision of opportunities to share the faith. When we reach that point in our lives, the impact that we make will not be limited to our company or to this age. Rather, we will touch the world for all of eternity.

Seeing the
Whole Man

DALE P. JONES
**President,
Halliburton Company**

T he reputation of the oil patch is that of a place of
hard-drinking and hard-living men. But, I am constantly amazed at the number of outstanding Christian
leaders that populate the companies of the oil field. Dale
P. Jones is president of the Halliburton Company head-
quartered in Dallas, Texas. He also serves as a director of
the American Petroleum Institute, the National Associa-
tion of Manufacturers, the Offshore Technology Conference, and the National Foreign Trade Council. His
expertise in oil field matters has made him one of the
leading oil field executives in the world. He is also a
committed Christian.

Jones suggests that faith creates such an environment
because of an attitude of sensitivity to the human relations aspect of the workplace. Sharing faith is not always
a matter of an overt, evangelistic witness. Instead, the
opportunities to let people know of the importance of
Christ occur when you develop an atmosphere where
other people want to talk to you about the concerns of
their life. In an environment of genuine care and concern, the addressing of spiritual needs can become a natural part of the workplace.

"At Halliburton we recognize that a job is just a part of people's lives. Therefore, great emphasis is put on the home life. We make sure that the work is structured so that our employees can have time with their children. We have discovered that maintenance of every part of a person's life—the physical, the spiritual, and the emotional—adds to their ability to perform as employees."

In these days of constant discussion about national health care and employer mandates, Halliburton has forged a healthcare partnership between management and employees. "We maintain a strong emphasis on the drug-free workplace," and encourage employees to live healthy lifestyles that recognize the relationship between health and all of their activities.

At the same time, however, Jones recognizes the opportunity and the obligation to share the gospel. That obligation begins with personal integrity and morality. "We cannot keep, on a long-term basis, separation between our word and our deed. If we profess Christianity, we have to show those values where we work." Even beyond the modeling of Christ in the marketplace, however, Jones finds that his position provides him a unique opportunity to share the gospel all around the world. "Whenever I travel internationally, I spend time with local evangelistic groups. The people in our company know what I am doing, so that opens even more doors for me. Whenever I travel in countries where there has not been much access to Scripture, I try to get involved with passing out Bibles. Sometimes we have to handle it very carefully—for instance, in China—and be sensitive to diversity, but usually we have found open arms wherever we try to take God's Word."

HOW MUCH HIGHER?

13

The day will happen whether or not you get up.
John Ciardi

I sat across the table from one of the world's foremost authorities on infectious diseases. Whenever an epidemic of unknown origin or type would break out, wherever it might be in the world, this was the man who would be called in to isolate and identify the problem. He had reached the pinnacle of his field. I came prepared to talk about some financial matters, but his first question caught me off guard. "Do you have family at home?" he asked. "Yes," I replied. "Then why are you here, halfway across the country from them?" he demanded. A bit taken aback, I responded that my job required that I be on the road much of the time.

"Then quit," he said. "It's not worth it. At the beginning of my career I decided that I was going to be the very best in my field, and I was going to do it for my family. But that meant long hours at the office, longer hours in the lab, and traveling all over the world to track down the latest exotic disease. Well, I reached the top. I'm one of the best in the world, and it has destroyed my family."

At some point in the lives of most executives, there comes a time when a choice must be made whether or not to pursue the next rung on the executive ladder, fully recognizing that the upward climb will mean a price must be paid by the family. Even that recognition of the conflict, however, does not give us an automatic answer. There are situations where the benefits of the new position far outweigh the costs exacted from the family. Most executives, at some time in their lives, have been called upon to make a major move with their family. Those moves can, at times, be disruptive for a household. But, the benefits of a better position, a continued relationship with the company, or improved working conditions can offset the drawbacks to the move. So, the answer does not come easily.

You will not find in this chapter an indictment of ambition or condemnation of the desire to gain a better position in the corporate world. What you will find, however, is an affirmation that Christian businessmen have an obligation before God to examine closely the motivations and priorities of life. When we lose that sense of divine balance, our world begins to come unglued, and our work, our family, and our church feel the consequences.

Drivenness

My attorney friend watched our eating companion walk away from the table to make a "quick phone call." He shook his head, "Boy, I'd love to have Mark working for me, but I'd surely hate to work for him. That is the most driven person I've ever known in my life." Blessed with slightly-above-average intellect and a modicum of talent, an incredible drive pushed him to an executive position in an international corporation while he was still a college student. When he graduated, a transfer and a big promotion were waiting. Mark is a successful businessman by anyone's standards. He is the kind of loyal employee most corporations only dream of having on the payroll. He is the first one to the office in the morning and the last one to leave at night, sometimes only catching a couple of hours sleep curled up in an overstuffed chair in the outer lobby of his office.

The only relationship that Mark has ever maintained in his life is the one with his business. Those of us who consider him our friend are able to make contact with him only once every year or two; he is estranged from his parents, and he's never been able to sustain a relationship with a woman for more than three or four months at a time. People are by and large extraneous; they just get in the way of his doing his job as he thinks he should. I have no doubt that it is fortunate Mark does not have a family, for if he did, a wife and children would find that they always played a secondary role in his life, never gaining the importance had by the office. To say that Mark is driven is an understatement.

While he is an extreme case, many of our corporations have ranks full of people who feel that their primary obligation is to the company, superseding in importance the family, the church, and the community. They are what we used to call workaholics.

Who knows what inner demons may drive these individuals? Some, perhaps, experienced poverty in their childhood, and they fight forever to keep the wolf away from the door. Others may have for some reason felt that they never measured up, and so they keep climbing, hoping one day to reach that pinnacle of success that will let them know they are no longer inferior.

People are always neglecting something they can do in trying to do something they can't.

—Ed Howe

We as believers need to understand that there is a great difference between being called and being driven. The individual who is called by God has a sense of his place in the world and how he fits into the big picture. The individual who is driven senses that he will never fit in anywhere in this world or the next, and, therefore, his life becomes an attempt to justify his existence.

In our twisted world, even drivenness is becoming a source of pride. A commercial for a leading automobile manufacturer ends with the slogan "we are driven." No executive seems to really be worth his corporate salt unless he can score over 200 on the Holme stress chart. And it's not just the big businessman who seems to have lost the balance and perspective on important things in life. I've known pastors, farmers, carpenters, as well as insurance salesmen and presidents of Fortune 500 companies who could never work quite hard enough.

Perhaps, to some degree, every successful person is driven. All of us want to climb; all of us want to better our lot in life. When ambition becomes the controlling force in our lives, however, then we know we've reached the danger zone. There are, fortunately, some danger signs along the way to let us know when we are about to pass the limit of safety:

1) *Driven individuals place greater priority upon achievement than on relationships.* In a driven person's life, people become objects rather than individuals, as we discussed in Chapter 5. For the driven individual, people become stepping stones to corporate achievement. Therefore, the individual is a failure at genuinely cultivating relationships; instead, he manipulates people to get what he wants. Gordon MacDonald refers to this as "a psychology of achievement." For the driven individual, gratification comes only with the accomplishment of goals, never in the journey along the way or in relationships developed within family, corporation, or community.

2) *Driven people tend to see everything in the context of win/lose.* The driven individual always wants to know the final score. He may claim that he is competing against himself, but that is almost always a rationalization to make him believe that he does not care what other people think. Don't be fooled; winning is all that counts. Beating everyone else is of ultimate importance because it is only in that manner that the driven individual

can show his superiority over everyone else. For the driven individual, the outcome is always in doubt, and even success is short-lived.

3) *Driven people are obsessed with the appearance of success.* More lies are told at class reunions than in any other place. We all want to look good, and we want our friends to think we have made it. We would like to drive the biggest car, go further, and climb higher than any of our old associates. Only a few mature personalities ever get beyond that need for gratification which comes from having other people think that they have "made it." For the driven individual, success in the eyes of others becomes the ultimate goal. He, therefore, becomes obsessed with accumulating those things that say power and prestige to everyone else. He wants the biggest car and the nicest house. For him, a woman is less a partner with whom life is shared than she is a trophy to be displayed. Ultimately, none of these things can ever provide the refuge which the driven individual seeks. Instead, the goal remains forever just beyond their reach. There is always something better, and he never reaches the pinnacle.

A Different Measure

Such a view of life is a far cry from the biblical perspective. We know we are of value because God loves us, not because of what we accomplish. We know the ultimate outcome has already been decided, and God has pronounced us victorious. Therefore, the journey becomes as important as the outcome. We are set free from always winning simply because we know that we are the ultimate victors. We can take time to develop relationships and enjoy the game as it is played. We can genuinely compete against ourselves because the goal that is stretched before us is to be the very best that we can be before God.

The Christian simply must not measure success in the same manner that the world does. We are held to a different—and much higher—standard. But, we seek to reach that standard not for gratuitous self-approval. Instead, we endeavor to reach the "high calling of Jesus Christ." Within the context of that perspective, then, ultimate success is less about winning than it is about faithfulness.

At What Cost?

The believer is to be forever diligent that the hounds of drivenness stay far from the door. At the same time, however, we recognize a responsibility to strive to be the best we can be, and there is nothing wrong with that desire. Indeed, we have a responsibility to continue to grow. It is a natural and productive impulse to seek to better our lot in life. Few companies even want employees who are completely satisfied with their position, not desiring to move up through the corporate ranks. Indeed, the very basis of our economic system is a competitive instinct among all in the workforce. The system itself seems to be at odds with New Testament morality. Can we as Christians effectively participate and yet maintain our integrity as followers of Jesus Christ?

Some men succeed by what they know; some by what they do; and a few by what they are.
—Elbert Hubbard

I think the operative word, as in so many other areas of this book, is *balance*. We need to recognize and tap that drive to be more than we have been in the past, but we also need to understand the bigger picture. When we do, we can effectively weigh the demands of the marketplace against our commitment to church and family.

We begin by asking ourselves the question of why we want to climb the corporate ladder. At the foundation of ambition is the human drive to achieve. Part of our creation is that urge to have dominion and to control. *That impulse, in and of itself, is not evil.* But, when the instinct to achieve becomes the driving thrust of all that we are, when it becomes the controlling and operative factor in life, then the gift of dominion that God has given us has become corrupted.

Climbing for the sake of climbing is acceptable only if our ambition is not incurring costs in other areas of our lives. In other words, if we do not need a promotion, if that promotion is of no value to us except to make us feel good about ourselves or to salve an ego, then we must insure that the climb is not taking its toll out of other areas of our life—most notably, in relationships.

On the other hand, there are many positive motives for desiring to move higher in the world. All of us desire to be able to provide comfortably for our families. Very often, a promotion will provide the means by which we can meet the financial needs of our family. Or, perhaps a larger paycheck will allow us to contribute more to an area of ministry.

In many situations, a promotion or a climb up the corporate ladder will put us in a position to make decisions or to accomplish something that would be of benefit to all. Perhaps it will be in directing the corporate philosophy in such a way as to bring greater good to the community or even in leading the company toward a growth pattern that would provide more positions for additional employees. Those are great reasons for a Christian to struggle, to compete for the better position.

At the same time, however, our reasons for seeking to move up in the world may be the very best, but the results of our drive to the top can be disastrous. A good friend of mine developed an innovative program which will be of great benefit to the fund-raising efforts of the charitable institutions of America. He saw the work that he did as a genuinely divine calling. After he developed the program, he reached an agreement with a nationally recognized firm to do the marketing.

Even after he turned the program over to them, however, he remained the company's obvious choice for the national director of the program. Such a position would have almost certainly meant a doubling or tripling of his salary. It would allow him to do many of the things for his family, his community, and his church that he probably had always wanted to do. However, he had two small children at home, and accepting leadership of this branch of the corporation would have meant three to four days a week on the road. He would have missed seeing his son and daughter grow up. Though experiencing the pain of separation that came when he had to let go of "his" program, knowing that probably no one could run it as well as he could, he let go of the reigns, and told the company no. His family was just too important. We can have all of the right motives for moving up in the world, and yet look around to find that the cost is simply more than we are willing to pay. At such a time, we are called on to make that hard decision and to accept the lordship of Christ in our life, the lordship that demands that we always place relationships before all other callings.

Learning to Say No

A friend related his business philosophy to me: "Don't ever tell them that you do not know the answer, and never turn down an assignment." Unfortunately, that is a perspective that is far too prevalent in the business community.

At the same time, however, there is a mentality in this country that says the only ones we can really say no to are those whom we love the most. We cannot refuse the company, but we can impose on the family. What ends up happening, then, is that our families make the sacrifices so that no one else needs to do so.

Interestingly enough, I see the problem in pastors perhaps more than in any other vocation. Most ministers seem to feel that no project of the work of God can possibly survive without

No one has ever better articulated what it means to give up the world's measure of success, to focus on the things that are really important, than did Albert Schweitzer. Ultimately, though, Schweitzer found all that he had sacrificed return to him:

"When I first went to Africa I prepared to make three sacrifices: to abandon the organ, to renounce the academic teaching activities to which I had given my heart, and to lose my financial independence, relying for the rest of my life on the help of friends.

"These three sacrifices I had begun to make, and only my intimate friends knew what they cost me.

"But now there happened to me, what happened to Abraham when he prepared to sacrifice his son. I, like him, was spared the sacrifice. The piano with pedal attachment, built for the tropics, which the Paris Bach Society had presented to me, and the triumph of my own health over the tropical climate had allowed me to keep up my skill on the organ. During the many quiet hours which I was able to spend with Bach during my four and a half years of loneliness in the jungle I had penetrated deeper into the spirit of his works. I returned to Europe, therefore, not as an artist who had become an amateur, but in full possession of my technique and privileged to find that, as an artist, I was more esteemed than before.

"For the renunciation of my teaching activities in Strassburg University I found compensation in opportunities of lecturing in very many others.

"And if I did for a time lose my financial independence, I was able now to win it again by means of organ and pen.

> *"That I was let off the threefold sacrifice I had already offered was for me the encouraging experience which in all the difficulties brought upon me, and upon so many others, by the fateful postwar period has buoyed me up, and made me ready for every effort and every renunciation."*

their input and often without their control. They make every committee meeting, every social function, and every activity of the church. Many church members, in whatever type of need—sickness, celebration, spiritual crisis—also seem to feel that only the pastor can make it right. Therefore, many ministers rarely eat a meal with their family. They miss their children's ball games. Their spouses are often already in bed when they come home at night. They have never learned to say no.

But this is not just a problem of the pulpit. It is also one that seems to greatly infect mid-level corporate executives. Perhaps the ones on the very top of the corporate ladder feel secure enough in their positions that they are comfortable with the occasional refusal. Those at the entry level may feel that they are insignificant enough that they can probably get by with demanding time for family and relaxation. Those in the middle are the ones stuck with this problem.

For many men, the problem is not deciding that saying no to demands made on personal time is the right response. They already know that is the right thing to do; it is just a matter of being able to do it. We fear the repercussions of being perceived as someone who will not give his all for the company. A no to an offered position might close the door to future advancement. And so we rightly have some degree of apprehension about refusing an assignment.

At the same time, however, most corporations understand that employees with full and well-rounded lives are the most productive members of the workforce. Most will have no problem when an individual turns down a position, especially if that individual has shown a steady and consistent history of really striving to be an effective employee. When a supervisor understands that a refusal is not arbitrary or just simple self interest, there is much less recalcitrance toward taking that no for an answer. So, by always saying yes, many men are actually providing something that the company has neither demanded nor really desires.

A Perspective on Position

One of my favorite hymns has the famous lines ". . . and whatever my lot, thou hast taught me to say, 'even so, it is well with my soul.'" Those lines bespeak a type of spiritual awareness that seems to be increasingly rare today. Our society has taught us to never be satisfied, no matter how high we have climbed. Indeed, sometimes the goal of advancement is irrelevant; we often climb simply for the sake of climbing rather than with any set purpose in mind.

When we seek to move up the corporate ladder, it must not be in a hope that a promotion or better position will bring ultimate satisfaction to us. If we are not happy "whatever our lot," then we cannot be happy in the very best of circumstances. Paul saw the situation quite well: "Not that I speak in regard to need, for I have learned in whatever state I am, to be content: I know how to be abased, and I know how to abound. Everywhere and in all things I have learned both to be full and to be hungry, both to abound and to suffer need" (Phil. 4:11–12).

One of the most important lessons of Scripture is that neither our attitude nor our activity is ultimately determined by our circumstance. We are to be faithful to God and have the peaceful awareness of his presence no matter where we stand in life. If our drive to the top is simply an attempt to get beyond the pain and the drudgery of everyday life, we will find no contentment in a better position.

I have found wondrously happy and satisfied individuals fulfilling their tasks in life in a competent and joyful manner even though they only appeared at the very bottom of the organization chart. At the same, we've all seen those people who have climbed to the very top and found no fulfillment in title, responsibility, or financial reward. Satisfaction is not ultimately a function of where we are; it is a result of who we are. Once we discover the joy that only exists in living life to its fullness in the presence of Jesus Christ, then we can say with the hymnist, "It is well with my soul."

Making the Commitment to Family

COLONEL RICHARD BIONDI
United States Army, Ret.

C olonel Richard Biondi (U.S. Army, Ret.) understands better than most the tension that can exist
between family and career. Colonel Biondi was at one
time the Senior U.S. Army Commander in Greece. He
served two tours in Vietnam at the height of the conflict.
In the midst of this, Colonel Biondi has remained a
committed husband, father, and churchman.

Few careers place greater demands on family relationships than does the military. Being an Army officer
means extended periods of separation from the family.
When his children were small, Colonel Biondi was sta-
tioned in Fort Polk, Louisiana. His duties required him
to leave home each morning at 5:15. Often, the children
were in bed when he returned in the evening. "We
would have dinner each evening at 7:00. If I was not
there, Paula would feed the children. I made it about 50
percent of the time."

Perhaps even more difficult were the extended periods
of separation. Families are not, of course, allowed into
combat zones, and Richard's daughter was born during
his second Vietnam tour. Almost as difficult for the family, though, are those regular peacetime deployments

which are a part of any soldier's life. While at Fort Polk, Richard participated in four deployments lasting from four to seven weeks. During those times, contact with his family was minimal.

And then there are those Army transfers. Regular moves are part of the career military family's life, and the experiences of the Biondi family were no exception. Several times during his daughter's teenage years, the family was required to relocate from the home and community into which they had just settled.

One of the most difficult moves came as his daughter entered high school. The family had been transferred to a base in Oklahoma where his daughter became reacquainted with some close friends from her early childhood. Richard had promised the family that there would be no more moves unless he was given the opportunity to become a Commander once again.

And then the call came. Colonel Biondi was offered the position of Commander of U.S. Army Forces in Greece. It was an offer he simply did not feel he could turn down. But, it meant removing his family from an environment in which they were comfortable and happy, and taking them halfway around the world. Leaving his family behind and accepting an unaccompanied tour was not an option for the Biondis.

"When we got to Greece, I made a promise to the family that the next assignment would be back to the United States. In my years in the service, I had never told the Army no before; I always felt that whatever my country asked of me, I should do. But after two years in Greece, I was being pressured to take another overseas assignment, and for the first time in my career, I resisted. After several months, it was agreed that I would be transferred to College Station, Texas, to serve as Professor of Military Science and Deputy Commandant for the Texas A & M University Corps of Cadets. My daughter was able to attend her last two years of high school back in the United States."

In spite of the difficult family situation with a father often absent and frequent unsettling moves, Richard and Paula Biondi have raised two children who display solid citizenship and solid values. How did they go about doing that? "I think the operative words are commitment and priority," suggests Colonel Biondi. "Paula and I were raised in the same type of families with the same type of values. We wanted the same things for our family. Values of right and wrong must be taught from early childhood, and we as parents must set high moral values by the way we lead our daily lives. Kids learn what they see. We must set a good example if we are to expect our children to possess these same high values." Richard suggests that it was his wife's commitment to the values of family that held them together during those times when he had to be away.

At the same time, his family situation required a special kind of commitment from him. "If the children had a play or a school program, I did everything within my power to be there. If it meant driving forty-five minutes to see a short play or school program, then driving forty-five minutes back to work, I did it when I could, and it was worth it." Children recognize that kind of faithfulness and commitment in our lives, and they respond to it. When our children understand that we are willing to make the sacrifices to see that the family functions as a family, they are given a sense of the importance of those relationships. At times, however, that commitment can mean making hard choices, choices that can be very costly in terms of a military career.

With his position as U.S. Army Commander in Greece, Colonel Biondi was moving into that small circle of elite officers who lead this country's military, and there was a strong likelihood that his next assignment could lead to his promotion to General Officer, the ultimate goal of any career military man. However, by refusing the positions that were offered and moving to Texas A & M University to become involved with the student Cadet Corps, the prospects for further promotion were eliminated. Colonel Biondi made a conscious decision of family over career. At the same time, however, he made the ultimate statement to his family of their priority in his life.

PASSING IT ON

14

And you, fathers, do not provoke your children to wrath, but bring them up in the training and admonition of the Lord.
Ephesians 6:4

What is the first thing you ask a recent college graduate who is applying for a job?" The question was addressed to the personnel director of a major corporation. "I want to know who paid for their college," began his reply. "The kid who worked to pay at least part of the college bills is miles ahead of the one who relied on Mom and Dad to take care of everything. He understands how to balance competing obligations. His college work was almost certainly not at an executive level, so he understands the viewpoint of the employee and doesn't expect to be treated like royalty. But most important, he has a sense of responsibility for his own success. That's what we need in our business."

A sense of responsibility for his own success. In other words, he has a work ethic. It seems that the older generation has always despaired about the values and work ethic of their successors. Socrates complained that the youth of his day were lazy and shiftless with no sense of right and wrong. Children of the fifties and sixties, who may have been the most criticized generation in all of history, look at the teenagers today and despair at the vulgar music, casual attitudes toward sex, and the random violence which marks the culture of the young.

■ ─────────────────────────────────────

You can't push anyone up the ladder unless he is willing to climb himself. —Andrew Carnegie

───────────────────────────────────── ■

I see those images on television, also, but they do not reflect the majority of the young people that I know. There are a lot of good kids out there, kids with sound heads on their shoulders, with solid moral values, and with the quality of persistence that keeps their lives on the right track.

And they did not get that way by accident. Instead, those qualities were cultivated in them by parents who understood the necessity of a work ethic. For the very best of this generation, work and responsibility have been part of their lives since early childhood.

Giving our children a sense of the worthiness of work is different from any other type of values development. Without question, all values are lifestyle choices. It is recognized that in all areas of life we sometimes face choices for which there are no clear, unambiguous responses: we should be truthful, we should not take property that does not belong to us, we should treat others kindly, we should return good for evil.

When we come to the issue of a work ethic, however, the lines are seldom cleanly drawn. What does it mean to have a work ethic? How is a work ethic lived out in our daily lives? Even when we answer the basic questions, the ethic itself engenders a great deal of tension. Is there any other area in which it is so easy to do the right thing for all of the wrong reasons? Throughout corporate America we have example after example of individuals who have outstanding work ethics but who are driven by an internal demon of power, greed, or insecurity.

We are, therefore, left with a dilemma in passing on a work ethic to our children. To be certain, we must teach them the necessity of striving to do their best, to contribute, to produce. At the same time, however, they must realize that the drive to genuine success can be so easily corrupted. Our obligation before God is to give our children a well-rounded and biblical understanding of what it means to be productive members of the workplace. That understanding is something that will stay with them for life.

A Model Worth Emulating

Continuing with our theme that "more is caught than is taught," the first step in helping our children gain an understanding of their place in the working world is to give them a model which is desirable and attractive.

I came on the real Goethe when it struck me in connection with his activities that he could not think of any intellectual employment without practical work side by side with it, and that the two were not held together by their character and object being similar, but were quite distinct and only united through his personality. It gripped me deeply that for this giant among the intellectuals there was no work which he held to be beneath his dignity, no practical employment of which he ever said that others on account of their natural gifts and of their profession could do it better than he, and that he was always ready to prove the unity of his personality by the union of practical work with intellectual activity. —Albert Schweitzer

There a lot of hardworking men in the workplace in America. There are also a lot of hardworking men who have given their children absolutely no reason to want to follow to a corporate desk or a carpenter's scaffold; their children have no desire to follow in their footsteps, for they project no sense of a work ethic. The only expression that the children hear is one of dread and drudgery. Although hard and conscientious laborers, be it in the office or on the job site, they do not communicate an appreciation for the task. On the other hand, some men take a genuine joy in their work, but the family can see the job only as something that takes Dad away from the kids, and the children grow resentful of the undue influence that work has in the life of the family.

The beginning point, then, is to give our children not just an example of what hard work is, but a model that is worthy of emulation. To communicate effectively what it means to have a sense of work, the model of workmanship that we demonstrate for our children must have three characteristics:

We must have a sense of enjoyment in our work. Work isn't always fun and games. Sometimes it is headaches, drudgery, and long hours. At the same time, however, if we have a healthy attitude toward work and a sense of calledness in our vocation, the natural result should be a genuine enjoyment in what we do. Children may sometimes have difficulty distinguishing between the challenges that are part of a task and genuine dislike of our work.

When our youngest was a first grader, she would sometimes walk into our room in the evenings when I was trying to get in a little exercise before going to bed. As she found me panting, grimacing, and straining through a long round of situps, she began to beg me to stop, pleading with me to quit hurting myself. It took some time before I convinced her that I really did enjoy the exercise and that it really was in my best interest.

In the same way, when our children see us wrestling with any difficult task, there is a tendency to equate difficulty with dislike. We must be very careful that, even in the midst of the

Nothing is more important than genuine commitment to a task. That commitment will be forever obvious to all who observe what we do, even if they cannot immediately articulate what they see as "commitment." Andre Soltner of Lutèce in New York puts it this way: "I am more than thirty years a chef. I know what I am doing and each day I do my absolute best. I cook for you from my heart, with love. It must be the same with service. The waiter must serve with love. Otherwise, the food is nothing. Do you see? Many times, I will leave my kitchen and go to the tables to take the orders myself. It starts right then and there . . . People ask me all the time what secrets I have. I tell them there is nothing mysterious about Lutèce. I put love in my cooking and love in the serving. That is all."

hardest task, we somehow convey a sense of joy in our work, whether it involves the office, the yard work, or the workshop. This is not a call for falseness, but a suggestion that we recognize the necessity of communicating that we enjoy what we do.

If a man goes into business with only the idea of making money, the chances are he won't.
—Joyce Clyde Hall

We must have a sense of purpose in our work. Children can most easily comprehend joy in our work when they see that we are doing something worthwhile. Younger children usually have very little concept of how what we do fits into the bigger picture of our business. They may know that we work at a bank or an insurance company or for a construction firm. What they often don't understand, however, is how what we do complements what everyone else does. When we begin to communicate to them a sense of accomplishment and purpose, we have gone a long way toward establishing a reason for our hard work. A work ethic begins with the understanding that we are not just laboring to bring home a paycheck or to occupy our time; rather, we are living out our lives as productive members of society. When children begin to grasp that fact, they begin to understand how what we do—and what they do—fits into the bigger picture.

We must have a sense of balance in our work. There are many men who have a great work ethic but who are absolutely rotten fathers. They are so consumed by their drive for success and accomplishment in their profession that they forget about their other responsibilities to their family.

Modeling that type of work ethic for children is worse than having no work ethic at all. The children will either reject work as taking away from the important parts of life, or, perhaps worse, approach work in the same manner, and destroy relationships in the same way.

What children need to see is a sense of balance and commitment, a recognition that work is a part of our lives—an important part certainly—but one that is balanced with all of the other obligations of family, church, and community. They also need to see a sense of joy and purpose in that balance which permeates *all* that we do, not just our hours at the office or our time at the work site. Instead, we live within that sense of joy and that sense of purpose, allowing it to touch all that we do. When work, then, becomes a component of the Christian lifestyle rather than a category set to itself, we have fully integrated a model worthy of emulation.

Christian Quality

I've always wanted to be a craftsman. I especially admire finely crafted wood, be it in furniture, architecture, or just a string of well-made decoys. To take a block of mahogany and with lathe, chisel, and carving knife turn it into a useful and beautiful project is a gift, though admittedly a gift developed through years of practice and faithful attention to a craft. Unfortunately, however, I have neither the skill, patience, nor artistic insight to coax the innate beauty out of a block of wood.

Perhaps it is just the Calvinist in me, but I can't help equating quality with Christianity. Not so much that I see something well done and immediately assume the one responsible for the project is a Christian, but rather that when I see work that is shoddily done, I question the moral virtue of its careless master. Without doubt, that is an unfair judgment, but I wonder if it is not an assumption shared by believers and non-Christians alike, one to which we ought to give some careful attention.

To be certain, no Christian is ever completely free of sin, and that certainly affects our workplace. Even those whom we would consider heroes of faith—Paul, Spurgeon, Carey, and others—spoke about the continual presence of sinfulness in their lives. Sin is also prevalent in the world, which means that even as we recognize work as a blessing of God, there may be certain aspects of it that simply are not pleasant. In all work, there is some element of exertion, unpleasantness, and demand. If every aspect of our work were enjoyable, we would all be great craftsmen.

Luther talked extensively about the relationship of sin to the vocation of work. He suggested that the faithful performance of the difficult requirements of our vocation is the way by which we give living example of dying with Christ through crucifixion. He states, "This takes place day by day through the putting to death of the old man and the rising of the new man out of sin. This is completely affected in death when the body of sin withers and God's new creation appears in consummation. The old man does not want to die. . . . God must help him to die daily. In one's vocation there is a cross, for prince, husband, father, daughter, for everyone, and on this cross, the old human nature is to be crucified. Under this cross are included the most trivial of difficulties, such as, in marriage, the care of babes which interferes with sleep and enjoyment; in government, unruly subjects and promoters of revolt; in the ministry, the whole resistance to reformation; in heavy labor, shabbiness, uncleanliness, and contempt of the proud. No person who lets the work of that vocation go forward without grudging will escape troubles, hatred, and persecution. The Christian is crucified by the law in his vocation."

According to Luther, when we as Christians give careful attention to the less enjoyable requirements of our work, we give evidence of the grace of God in our lives. Indeed, we may even look at those difficult aspects of our work as "the law from which Christ has set us free." God's grace, then, allows us to fulfill its requirements without being captured by its penalty. As Augustine wrote, "The law was given in order that grace might be sought; grace was given in order that the law might be fulfilled."

The moral attributes are not a given in our life. They do not automatically appear and thrust themselves upon the stage of our lives. Instead, we are called upon to exert the effort, and the fact that they do require effort by no means lessens the grace aspect of them. Recognizing the greatness of God's gift does not automatically make it all easy. Rather, that grace gives us the moral power to progress toward Christian quality.

Paul is the theologian of grace. When we look at his writings in the New Testament, we are almost overwhelmed by his picture of a God who comes to us not because of our good works, but in spite of our sinfulness. At the same time, however, Paul constantly gave evidence of an understanding that effort was to be exerted in all that we do. Paul said, "For by grace you have been saved through faith, and that not of yourselves; it is the gift of God, not of works, lest anyone should boast."

Such an understanding of the biblical teaching of the necessity of continued effort on the part of a Christian gives rise to a theology of quality. When we as men of God take seriously the activity of grace in our lives, we are bound by that grace to return a faithful and careful effort *for the purpose of the service of God.* Indeed, if our work ethic is founded upon the premise that God has given us a stewardship of dominion, then our work must be reflective of both duty to God and our recognition of God's own wise craftsmanship.

We are, first of all, bound by divine calling to do whatever work we do "as unto God." This means that whatever task is undertaken—from the top to the bottom of the corporate ladder—must be done as if it is being presented to God, for in a very real sense, it is.

Just as important, our Creator-God in his crafting of the world has given us a pattern for our work. One of the most intriguing statements in all of Scripture is when God looked at his newly formed creation and "saw that it was good." This is an overt statement of God's own pride in his work. We, therefore, who are called to be partners with God in the development of this world which he has formed have an obligation toward that original creation to be able to look at our own work and say, "It is good." The work of God demands nothing less from us.

In a very real sense, then, our work becomes witness to both the type of God we have as well as to our faithfulness toward him. When we show shoddy workmanship in any task that we undertake, be it that of worship on Sunday morning, or the completion of an annual report, we have told the world that we are not at all taking seriously our faith.

To no less extent, we gain the moral authority to speak to the issues of our day when we show the world that we take quality very seriously. Far too often, the evangelical community has failed to put its best foot forward by showing the quality of who we are by the work that we do. Many other groups have stepped into the vacuum of quality that we have often left open.

I recently saw a national study which listed Utah as one of the best places in the country to take a manufacturing business. Utah received its ranking because of: 1) a high-quality available workforce, and 2) a positive living environment. Who was responsible for those conditions? Quite simply, the Mormon church. The Mormons have inculcated in their people an awareness of the importance of quality in all that they do. Therefore, they take that drive for quality not only to their homes and their schools but also to their places of work, and it makes a difference in the way the world perceives them.

Some of the most attractive advertisements on television today are those produced by the Mormon church. Very often, they show attractive families in attractive homes talking about the importance of faith and values in their lives. These ads are singularly well done. If I were an individual searching for answers in my life and I saw that type of production, I know I would be attracted to it.

Why do we as an evangelical community not have the same reputation for quality? We are the heirs of a great tradition that stretches all the way back to biblical times. We can reclaim that tradition when we begin to take very seriously the obligation to produce quality in all that we do, when we begin to do all labor as unto God.

Small Steps

It would be nice if we could just set a good example and leave it at that, wouldn't it? If we could only set our course in life and do what's right, knowing that our children would follow properly behind us. Children can be great mimics, but simple imitation of even the best model does not inscribe values into the character of a child. Our modeling must be followed by teaching. That teaching must be done in a manner which not only produces the desired result, but also produces the desired motivation—and that may be the most difficult aspect.

There must be a level of intentionality in our efforts to help our children gain a sense of the value of work. Just as within any good business plan, we must take concrete steps toward a stated objective. It probably does not hurt to give ourselves some interim grades along the way and to check for deficiencies in the process.

> *Manual labor to my father was not only good and*
> *decent for its own sake, but, as he was given to*
> *saying, it straightened out one's thoughts, a conten-*
> *tion which I have since proved on many occasions;*
> *indeed, the best antidote I know to a confused*
> *head or to tangled emotions is work with one's*
> *hands. To scrub a floor has alleviated many a*
> *broken heart and to wash and iron one's clothes*
> *brought order and clarity to many a perplexed*
> *and anxious mind.*   —Mary Ellen Chase
>   *A Goodly Fellowship*

Work must not be a bad word. The integrating concept in any instruction we give our children about work—be it modeling, object lesson, or practical experience—is that work is not something to be dreaded or avoided. Rather, work, though sometimes difficult, is a genuinely positive part of our everyday experience.

Admittedly, that can be a tough sell, whether it is to a first grader or a teenager, but it is a critical concept that must be cultivated throughout the years of childhood. We must begin developing a work ethic in our children at a very early age. As soon as a child is old enough to have some concept of responsibility, privilege, and obedience, the child needs to understand that tasks are a part of daily life.

Robert Fulghum's classic, *Everything I Really Needed to Know, I Learned in Kindergarten,* may be the best primer ever written about gaining a work ethic. He lists the responsibilities placed upon a child at an early age: put things back where you found them; clean up your own mess; flush. The child who, at an early age, has begun to master those simple assignments of life has laid a firm foundation for productivity as an adult.

Just as they need to understand why we do what we do, children also need a sense of purpose in their tasks. A "because

I said so" is sometimes the only possible response to insistent queries about the why of an assignment. At the same time, however, whenever possible, we should help our children to understand the rationale behind what they do, whether we are discussing the purpose of keeping rooms clean or doing homework before watching cartoons.

■ ───

The reason a lot of people do not recognize opportunity is because it usually goes around wearing overalls looking like hard work.   —Thomas Edison

─── ■

One of the most important things that we can do toward instilling a work ethic in our children is to help them develop a sense of pride in their craftsmanship. School projects that are thrown together at the last minute, bedroom floors cleaned by stuffing everything in the closet, or even sloppy eating habits show a disregard for quality. While we do not mistake manners for morality, children do need a sense of pride in all that they do. When we encourage them to do their best, to really clean up their floor (instead of rearranging the mess), to do a project that shows their capabilities, to use the kind of manners that they know to use, then we are helping them to develop a sense of competence and resulting self-confidence in their own abilities.

Basic to the self-esteem of any child is this type of self-confidence that grows from a feeling of competence. Numerous studies have demonstrated that children who master a craft or a skill gain a level of self-confidence that carries over into the other arenas of their lives. If you genuinely want to instill a work ethic, one of the most effective things you can do is find a hobby to share with your child. As the child begins to gain expertise from the hours spent mastering a craft or developing detailed knowledge about a collection, the child gains a sense of the worthiness of effort. When Dad is participating with the

LBE (Leader by Example)

In an open memorandum sent to the "outside directors and trustees of all the organizations not in the Fortune 1000," Robert Townsend posed one question: "Ask yourself if you have a leader as a CEO." It's a good question to ask in our families too.

LBE	*Non-Leader*
Participates	Instructs
Listens	Talks
Makes the sacrifice to be present	Finds any excuse to be absent
Encourages independent thinking	Demands uniform answers
Recognizes different people need different responses	Treats everyone the same
Prays with his children	Reminds his children to pray
Watches *Three Stooges* and *Mac-Neil/Lehrer*	Watches *Crossfire* and *MacNeil/Lehrer*
Requires his children to work with him at tasks that will stretch their abilities	Decides it's easier to do it himself
Has strong convictions	Believes what is convenient
Trusts	Doubts
Pushes to grow	Protects from risks

child in those efforts, it becomes the best of both worlds. Not only is the work ethic modeled; it is also experienced.

Avoiding the Success Fantasy

We have all seen the worst-case scenario. The twelve-year-old Little League pitcher, driven to win, turns and screams at the shortstop who misses the bad bounce single off his glove.

When he gets home after a loss, his self-esteem is so tied to his success that he can't admit that he really didn't have as much on his fastball today. Instead, "The ump really missed that call at the plate; the kid never touched home. I don't know why the coach lets Steve play; he never does any good for our team anyway."

Oh, and where were his parents? They were the ones in the stands constantly berating the umpire, the other team's parents, or anyone else who they perceived as interfering with their son's success. And, they weren't any easier on their own son either. They wanted to know why he wasn't "bearing down."

■

The only place where success comes before work is in the dictionary.　　　　　　　　　—Vidal Sassoon

■

It is not enough that our children understand that work is important and that they have the inner drive necessary to be productive members of society. They must also have an understanding of what success genuinely is. What we want for our children is not success the way the world measures it, but a value system that teaches the virtue of responsibility.

We, as followers of Christ, simply do not have the prerogative of measuring success as the world does. It is simply not allowed. Life is not all about winning, coming out on top, or monetary achievement. Instead, it's about faithfulness. It is about setting our standards by those of our Lord. We are not called upon to finish first; we are called upon to finish faithful.

Expectations

We have all seen the headlines—a child achieves success on the big screen or on the tennis court by the time he reaches puberty. As the story unfolds, we often discover that the child has been pushed to such a place of remarkable achievement by a parent who recognized the latent talent and would not allow the child to do anything less than climb to the top. Indeed, the terms stage mother and tennis father have become recognized parts of our vocabulary.

Sadly, very few of these children ever develop into emotionally whole adults. Instead, the well-rounded personality is sacrificed for a tightly drawn circle which focuses on developing competitive fire or special talent. The children never have the time to learn the skills they need for survival in the real world. Because all with whom they come in contact have for so long focused on meeting the child's needs, they are simply incapable of functioning as productive members of the community. Most of those kids end up as big-time losers.

Admittedly, that's the extreme. It applies only to those rarest of rare individuals with extraordinary talent. At the same time, however, many parents have expectations for their children in terms of productivity and conduct that are simply unrealistic or at least not in the best interest of the child. Children are not miniature adults. They are, by and large, not capable of doing things as well as adults can do them. Most children cannot master new tasks as quickly as can adults (with the exception of computer games!). So, we cannot hold them to the standards of performance or behavior to which we hold ourselves.

What we can and should do, however, is develop in our children a sense of anticipation of excellence. That is, we should look at the tasks they are assigned and expect them to do those tasks as well as their abilities will allow. In other words, we teach our children to approach work with the same type of integrity with which we approach work.

We do not push children beyond their limits. Instead, we praise them for fulfilling potential and for stretching the boundaries.

Life in the Big Picture

At some point, children need to come to understand that work is a privilege given us not just by God, but also by the efforts of the other people who are productive members of our society. As they develop that understanding, they must also recognize the responsibility to return value to the community. Children are never too young to be exposed to volunteerism. In their earliest years, they need to see Mom and Dad working to make the church and the community a better place by their labors—labors for which they do not receive monetary compensation. By the time they are school age, they need to be involved in community service themselves.

There are ways to engender the spirit of service to the community. For the child already engaged in some type of profit activity, to do at least some of that same type of work simply out of service to others is a good place to start. For example, if an adolescent boy has a lawn service, his regular yards could include not only those for which he gets paid each week, but also the yards of one or two elderly individuals who are on fixed incomes and not able to pay. By so doing, a child can really begin to see the big picture of how it all fits together.

Developing this mind-set of service is indeed a difficult task. But perhaps, you can think of it as an investment; perhaps your child will be ready to share the responsibility of paying the bills by the time he reaches college.

MODELING CHRIST

15

God is dead.
Nietzsche, 1885

Nietzsche is dead.
God, 1900

Few Christian books have been wider read than the classic by Charles Sheldon, *In His Steps*. This novel tells the story of a town that is absolutely transformed when its Christian population begins to take seriously the moral and social demands of the gospel. The operative question for every situation encountered is, "What would Jesus do?"

The new paradigm absolutely revolutionizes their town. Within the answer to that question, the townsfolk find the response to the social ills of their community. The poor are no longer the forgotten segment of society, relationships are enhanced, and provisions for the genuine needs of others become a priority for the town. The town is no longer a collection of people; it is genuinely a community.

To be sure, Sheldon paints a utopian vision. With the possible exception of a small group of the early church in Jerusalem, no sizeable population has ever achieved community in that sense, for not even the local church has reached a consensus of behavior as it is depicted in the novel. At the same time, how-ever, the book is a powerful reminder that the message of Christ, applied in the situations of everyday life, transforms relationships at all levels.

The achievement of that kind of ethic has by and large remained a utopian dream for the Christian community. What has been realized time and time again within the community, however, is the emergence of those individuals who live in constant and consistent faith. Their witness elevates the entire body. Time and again, men and women of God have asked the question, "What would Jesus do?" as they face the situations of life. And in so doing, they have consistently modeled the type of ethic that transforms not only their lives, but the lives of all those around them—in their businesses, in their homes, in their churches, and in their communities.

The God Who Provides

We should remember the Old Testament lesson that the God of Israel was called "the God who provides" (Gen. 22:14). There is, perhaps, no more telling portrait of God because the story of Scripture is constantly a story of God's provision in spite of fallenness. Actually, "in spite of fallenness" is not even the right way to phrase it. Instead, we should say, "in the midst of and because of fallenness." Countless times the people of Israel found themselves simply incapable of living within the framework that God had established for them. Time and time again, God made provision for their fallenness.

From the very beginning, when Adam and Eve fell in the Garden, God made provision and drew a protective covenant with them for their lives outside of Eden. Perhaps the greatest promise in the Old Testament (outside of the promise of the Messiah) was God's statement to the Children of Israel: "You shall be a nation of priests." But the people of Israel were not even able to live up to that gift. They were not able to relate to God in a one-on-one manner; so in their fallenness, he provided a tribe of priests who would make intercession for them and plead their case before God. Even the ultimate revelation of God in Jesus Christ occurred as a provision for our fallenness and sin. While fallenness is never God's intent, it's always the avenue by which he proves his graciousness.

Our world is a fallen world, and our responses to it are imperfect. Each one of us sets out on many different courses during life and seemingly arrive at few destinations. The task of carrying Christ into the marketplace, of maintaining a faithful witness at home, of sustaining churchmanship during a time when churches are often held in disrepute, is a task fraught with difficulty. But it is the task to which God calls us, and it is a task for which he makes constant provision.

In the Image of God

We have talked off and on throughout this book about different Christian movements, and especially about the monastics. The church-sponsored movement known as monasticism arose during the early Middle Ages. No one can criticize the goal of the monastics: to be imitators of Christ. In everything they did, they attempted to create a lifestyle which would reflect the righteousness of Jesus Christ. They sought purity. They sought cleanliness. They sought holiness. They attempted to bring the whole of Christianity into reality in their lives.

At no time and no age has anyone carried the concept of devotion to Christ further than did the monastics. Their writings of contemplative devotional literature remain the greatest ever written. They set worthy standards of focused, righteous living.

Great idea. Bad plan. One look at the great medieval cathedrals paints for us a portrait of the mind-set which doomed the monastics. The inside of the cathedral is a place of austere and sacred beauty. It is altogether an appropriate place for the worship of God. On the outside of the great cathedrals, demons and gargoyles peek and hide among the vaults and buttresses.

The architecture reflects the mind-set of the time. That which was inside the wall of the church was deemed to be pure, holy, and reserved for God. The outside world, however, was seen as a place of great evil and great darkness.

The monastics, therefore, in order to remove themselves from the influence of such evil, sequestered themselves within the walls of the monastery. Indeed, our term *cloistered,* which refers to the monastery, is now used as a verb meaning "to separate or pull away."

Ultimately, the separation by which they sought to preserve their righteousness became that which destroyed them. The monastics practiced a private Christianity. Because of the evil they saw to be so pervasive in the world, they cloistered themselves, withdrawing from society so as to avoid contamination. But that separation meant that they could have no redeeming impact on their society.

We are called to take our faith not only to our home and church but to the workplace and to the community around us. We are to be an active part of society. For too long, the church has misunderstood the command, "Be in the world, but not of the world" to say, "Be of the world, but not in it." We need an engaging Christianity.

Do We Really Have to Take the Ten Commandments Seriously?

One thing I really like about God: he doesn't beat around the bush. He gets to the heart of the matter almost immediately. Take the Ten Commandments, for example. There it is, right there at the beginning: "You shall have no other gods before Me." There it is in black and white. Pretty cut-and-dried, isn't it?

If you were to ask any Christian to prioritize his or her life, I simply cannot imagine anybody ranking God second or third or further down the list. Of course he comes first. Or at least that's what statistical studies show.

But what do our actions show? It seems that we have always done a pretty good job of pushing him down the list. Consider the children of Israel in the wilderness, for example. There at Mt. Sinai, as soon as Moses was gone for a few hours, God finished a distant second to a golden calf. Centuries later, the prophet Haggai had to pronounce judgment on Israel as a harlot. And when John had his vision on the Isle of Patmos, some of the most striking words from the angel of the Lord are ". . . you have left your first love."

And it really didn't get much better in the years to follow. Throughout the centuries, men and women who claim the description of Christian have placed ceremony, icons, and even Scripture itself above the worship of God. Mankind really has trouble with this priority thing. Many in our contemporary society claim to be Christians yet still pursue the idols of fame, success, and corporate achievement. We often check our morality at the office door.

I once came very close to entering into a business partnership with a man who was a deacon in the church where I attended. As negotiations started, I stated—somewhat piously, no doubt—that I wanted our business propositions to be based on the moral principles of our faith. This good deacon first laughed at me, then told me I didn't know what I was talking about. At least he was right about that part: I did not have a clue what that commitment would entail. But the intent of his statement was quite different. He felt that there was no place in a business for consideration of Christian principles. Then he told me that if such was my business perspective, I needed to look for a partner elsewhere. Fortunately for both of us, the deal fell through.

Not making an idol out of the corporation means putting God's considerations in front of business considerations. Sometimes that may mean some choices, like Truett Cathy determining that Chick-fil-A would not do business on Sunday. At other times it may speak to the integrity of the way we approach our relationships with our employees and with other corporations. More than anything else, it means that we change the way we measure success. Ultimate success in Scripture is measured only by faithfulness to God.

The bottom line is, of course, important to any corporation. But when that bottom line is achieved through ways that are harmful to the spirit and soul, there is no measure of success in our dealings. Some corporations demand a loyalty which almost equals a religious devotion to the job. They may deny that they would ever ask you to put your job ahead of your commitment to God and family, but they wouldn't be very understanding if you turned down a promotion because a company transfer would not be in the best interest of your family.

It is easy to take potshots at the guy who has made his business his god. But that first commandment applies to the family also. Wait a minute. I thought devotion to your family was one of the central teachings of Scripture. It is. But, we answer to *God* first.

Our families are critically important to the well-being of individuals, the church, and society as a whole. But, we have to remember that even family is not an end unto itself. It is a means to the end. That end is relationship with other people and relationship with God. Unless we make God first in our life, the family relationship cannot be what it should be.

I have seen it happen too many times. Those situations when loyalty to family stood in the way of loyalty to God. Too many parents have on blinders when it comes to their own children. Out of misunderstood love or a misplaced sense of doting, they allow children to do things that don't bring honor to God. In so doing, they think they are acting in the best interest of their family. But anytime we deny the lordship of Christ in our lives or allow the lordship of Christ to be denied in the lives of other members of our family, we hurt the family itself.

So what's the big picture? It really gets back to the same thing we talked about in the first two chapters of this book. As God designed it, there are no conflicts between business and righteousness, between family and holiness. Instead, our honest labor should bring a sense of accomplishing the task of God, a sense of fulfilling his commands. Likewise, that which we do as part of the family in creating and redeeming life should be seen as obedience to God in fulfilling the larger plan that he has drawn for this world. In so doing, we fulfill righteousness.

Never in the history of the world have Christian men had the opportunity to influence so many others. Until the latter half of the twentieth century, the average man met only a handful of people during his lifetime. With the advent of modern communication, travel, and large corporations, many of us come into contact with more people in a week than our grandfathers did in a year. Each one of those persons represents an opportunity for us to be a witness of the gospel of Christ.

Probably one of the most misunderstood passages in Scripture is the Great Commission, and especially its closing promise, ". . . and lo, I am with you always, even to the end of the age." When we read that passage, we often see the Christian's mission as a perilous journey which we anticipate with foreboding fear. Our only comfort is the promise that no matter how perilous the journey may become, we will have Christ's presence to make provision and protect us.

The bottom line is heaven.
—Edwin H. Land

I do not think that's what the Great Commission is about at all. In the New Testament, the right to evangelize was seen as a great privilege—God had chosen to share the task of redeeming others with us. The words of Jesus are not the assignment of a terrible task; rather, they promise the right to participate in God's redeeming activity. This is a statement that God intends to share with us the right of calling others to salvation—and that he will join us in the joyful task.

We even misconstrue Jesus' promise of power to Peter in Matthew 16:18: ". . . and on this rock I will build My church, and the gates of Hades shall not prevail against it." That is not a fortress mentality, at least not on our side. The church of God is not pictured as that which is backed into a corner and fighting for survival. Instead, it is pictured as that which is moving forth throughout the world, breaking down the walls of fear, hatred, and distrust. Let's not forget: we're the ones on the offensive. We have a unique opportunity in America today to be faithful witnesses to the redeeming power of God in our actions, in our countenance, and in our words.

I said in the beginning of this writing that this was not a "you can have it all" book. But maybe it is, especially if we define *all* as being what God has in mind for us. Many men are already transforming the workplace. For them, it's no longer the rat race, the corporate jungle, or the survival of the fittest. Instead, it is the arena of God's grace and God's love just as surely as are the cloistered walls of the monastery. Men everywhere are discovering that the office need not destroy the family, that New Testament reality doesn't wipe out profits, and that a worker can still be productive while maintaining priorities in the home.

This whole idea of work ethic and the corporation grew out of legitimate Christian concerns. Concerns for provision, for stewardship, and for a partnership with God. Today, often with great justification, the corporation is seen as a heartless, soulless, incarnation of evil. At the same time, families are disintegrating and churches are declining. Could it be that junk bond schemes and broken families have at their root the same maladies? Could it be that corporate espionage and empty pews reflect the same lack of values? Could it be that the need for preemployment lie detector tests and prenuptial agreements are reflective of the same moral malaise?

It is time to reclaim America. Throughout history, God has given men positions of spiritual authority and attendant responsibility. There is a spiritual power available when men of

God determine before God and before one another that they will be faithful to his commands. It is time we took God seriously.

All that is not Christ, to me, is loss.

About the Author

David Z. Nowell received his Ph.D. in historical theology from Baylor University where he is an officer in university relations. David is also an ordained Baptist minister and lives with his wife, Susan, and two stepdaughters, Jinnifer and Meredith, in Waco, Texas. He has also written *Stepparent Is Not a Bad Word*.